# *THE CELEBRATION OF HOLY MASS*

# The Celebration of Holy Mass

A practical manual based on the revised Roman Missal and other official documents and instructions

by
Louis G. Hileman
T.O.R.

# LUMEN CHRISTI PRESS
Houston, Texas 77019

## COMMENDED

I have examined the manuscript "THE CELEBRATION OF HOLY MASS" and found it quite correct.

It will prove a valuable aid to those priests who desire to celebrate Holy Mass with fitting decorum, with dignity and with precision.

Congratulations for the well-spent effort.

Vatican City
September 23, 1974

✠ A. Bugnini
Titular Archbishop
of Diocletiana

## IMPRIMI POTEST

Silver Spring, Md.
November 11, 1974

Fr. Emil Gentile T.O.R.
Minister Provincial

## IMPRIMATUR

By virtue of the study afforded "THE CELEBRATION OF HOLY MASS" by His Excellency, the Most Reverend Annibale Bugnini, Titular-Archbishop of Diocletiana and Secretary of the Sacred Congregation for Divine Worship, and of His Excellency's resulting commendation, I am gratified in issuing the necessary Imprimatur for the publication of this work. In so doing, I join my own congratulations to those of the Archbishop for Father Hileman's research and welcome sharing in a significant area touching so intimately the heart of the Church's sound liturgical life.

Given at the
Diocesan Center
November 14, 1974

✠ James J. Hogan
Bishop of Altoona-Johnstown

Dedicated
to
Mary Immaculate
Mother of all priests

# Contents

| | |
|---|---:|
| Preface | ix |
| Mass with a Congregation | 1 |
| Communion under both Kinds | 55 |
| The Deacon | 61 |
| The Lector | 67 |
| The Acolyte | 71 |
| The Thurifer | 77 |
| Concelebration | 81 |
| Mass without a Congregation | 101 |
| Mass Joined with an Hour of the Divine Office | 115 |
| Appendix | 119 |
| Official Sources | 147 |
| Index | 149 |

## ABBREVIATIONS

| | |
|---|---|
| Gen. Instr. | General Instruction on the Roman Missal |
| C.S.L. | Constitution on the Sacred Liturgy |
| O.M. | The Order of Mass |
| IEW | Instruction on Eucharistic Worship |
| C.D.W. | Congregation for Divine Worship |
| E.R. | Holy Communion and Eucharistic Worship Outside Mass |

Acknowledgement. Illustrations of the key positions of the priest at Mass with a Congregation used with permission of CATHOLIC BIBLE PUBLISHERS, Wichita, Kansas; at Mass in Private courtesy of Franciscan Fathers, Hollidaysburg, Pa.

Library of Congress Catalog
Card Number: 76-12007

ISBN 0-912414-23-5

Printed in the United States of America

# Preface

In *Mediator Dei*, Pope Pius XII discussed the science of the liturgy, saying, among other things, that "it must conform to what the Church out of the abundance of her wisdom teaches and prescribes". In concluding the same encyclical, the Pontiff prayed: "May God, whom we worship and who is not the God of dissension but of peace, graciously grant to us all that during our earthly exile we may with one mind and one heart participate in the sacred liturgy".

Pope Paul VI re-echoed the same thought when, in introducing the Roman Missal revised in accord with the Decree of Second Vatican Council, he expressed the hope that ". . . it (the revised Missal) would be received by the faithful as a help and witness to the common unity of all".

The purpose of this manual is to further the desired-for 'unity with one mind and one heart', by providing the celebrant of Mass, and the other ministers of the sanctuary, with the ritual elements for the Eucharistic celebration. The manual brings together under one cover and in a manner easily understood the norms that have been formulated by the legitimate authority of the Church and which, to date, are found in several pamphlet-form Instructions. It is hoped that this manual will prove useful especially in the average parish church and religious oratory where the full complement of ministers may not be readily or always available.

The manual makes no mention of pontifical ceremonies, since the revised Caeremoniale Episcoporum is on the way. Neither does it describe Masses for Special Groups, Masses in the Home or Masses with Children, since the respective Instructions for these occasions, in which the formality of the parish or community Mass may be somewhat relaxed, give ample indication of what is permitted and local diocesan guidelines further detail them.

The reverent observance of the Church's ceremonies, which are intended to enhance the celebration of Holy Mass and to serve for the honor and the worship of God, will fulfill Pope Paul's expressed desire that "one single prayer will rise as an acceptable offering to our Father in heaven, through our High Priest Jesus Christ, through the Holy Spirit".

My deep gratitude is due to Archbishop Bugnini for his review and endorsement of the manuscript. My thanks, too, to Father Richard J. McNamara, T.O.R., chaplain to the Hollidaysburg State Hospital, for his encouragement, valuable comments and assistance in preparing the material.

LOUIS G. HILEMAN, T.O.R.

# Mass With A Congregation
## PREPARATIONS

There are three separate locations in the sanctuary where particular parts of the Mass are celebrated. These are, in the order of their use, the CHAIR, the AMBO, the ALTAR.

In the revised rite of Mass each of these places has a distinct role to play, which develops a sense of movement to the altar and leads to the Eucharistic action in the celebration. The chair, the place of presidency, symbolizes the role of the priest as the leader of the community; the altar, the place of sacrifice, symbolizes the celebrant's role as the minister-representative of Christ, who "does the same thing the Lord Himself did"; the *ambo*, the Table of the Word, is where the lector and the deacon read the Scripture lessons and the petitions of the prayer of the faithful. It may be used also by the celebrant for the homily.

The chair should be an individual one and clearly visible to all, for it is the celebrant alone who presides over the entire assembly. The sacramentary is placed near the chair. A microphone at the chair will enable the congregation to hear fully the priest's voice. The priest occupies the chair for the greeting and penitential rite, for the *Kyrie*, the *Gloria* and the opening prayer. He remains at the chair during the Liturgy of the Word, including the profession of faith and the prayer of the faithful. If, in the absence of the lector or deacon, he reads the lessons, he does so from the ambo. He may use the ambo for the homily.

There should be only one *ambo* in the sanctuary, and all the readings should be proclaimed from it. It should be a fixed ambo, not a mere portable lectern, and be placed where those who read from it can be easily heard and seen by all. The *ambo* should not be used by any minister other than the lector and the deacon;; it should not be used by the commentator, musician or other persons. The lectionary, if it is not carried in the entrance procession, should be on the ambo and opened at the appropriate place.

The altar, the symbol of Christ present in His Church, is covered with a white cloth. At least two wax candles are placed on or near the altar, but four or six may be used. Nothing else should be on the mensa until the Liturgy of the Eucharist begins (the bookstand, chalice, etc., should be on the credence table). The larger crucifix that dominates the altar area or the one carried in the entrance procession and placed near the altar, eliminates the need for a small one on the mensa. In any case, the corpus should face the congregation. If the Book of Gospels is carried by the deacon in the entrance procession, it is placed by him on the altar. It will be taken by him to the ambo after he has received the celebrant's blessing just before the Gospel.

The cruets of wine/water, the altarbreads in a

proper vessel (ciborium, paten or intinctorium), and the other items that will be carried by the faithful in the procession of gifts, should be readied on a stand at the rear of the church. The chalice[1], with the purificator, corporal and pall (if used), is prepared at the credence table and covered with a veil of the same color as the Mass vestments, or it may always be white. The basin and simple ewer with water and the towel, to be used at the Lavabo, are readied on the credence table. The bookstand, if it is needed to hold the sacramentary at the altar, is placed on this table, and the handbell, if used.

If the rite of blessing and sprinkling holy water is to take place, the vessel of water and the vessel of salt (if used) are made ready near the chair, or at another appropriate place. The people should have a complete view of this rite.

The vestments are prepared in the sacristy. For the celebrant: amice, alb, cincture, stole and chasuble of the color proper to the celebration[2]. For the deacon: the amice, alb, cincture, stole and dalmatic of the color proper to the celebration. On occasions of lesser solemnity the dalmatic may be omitted. To conform with the provesions of the Missal and the directives of the Episcopal Conference, the stole is worn by the celebrant and by the deacon UNDER the chasuble/dalmatic[3].

---

[1] The chalice is not carried in the procession of gifts, unless it is being presented to the church for the first time, or unless the wine for the Mass is already in the chalice.

[2] See Color of Vestments in appendix, n. 2.

[3] Cfr. Gen. Instr., nn. 299-300 and Newsletter, Aug. 1970, p. 2.

The Entrance Procession of the ministers and the priest.

For the (installed) acolyte: if a seminarian, the alb or surplice to be worn over the cassock or religious habit; if a layman, as determined by the Ordinary. The lector wears the vesture determined by the Ordinary of the place.

In any form of the Mass, when the proper minister carries the Scriptures in procession, whether at the entrance or at the Gospel, the minister should hold the Book elevated with both hands at about face-level, as a sign of the importance and the veneration that the Church gives to the written Word of God.

The priest does well who recites devoutly each day the prayers of Preparation for Mass and of Thanksgiving after Mass which are found in the appendix of the new sacramentary.

# INTRODUCTORY RITES

A few minutes before the Mass is to begin, the servers light the candles at the altar.

An entrance procession should normally begin the celebration. On Sundays (at the principal Mass at least) and on other more solemn occasions this procession should move through the church to the sanctuary.

The procession forms in the sacristy in this order: servers and acolytes, other ministers and clergy, lector, deacon, celebrant. A cross-bearer, flanked by two servers carrying lighted candles, may lead the way. When incense is used, the thurifer walks at the head of the procession[4]. If desired, either the Book of Gospels, held by a deacon, or the lectionary, held by the lector, may be carried in the procession, but not the sacramentary.

During the procession an appropriate hymn may be sung; otherwise the given antiphon of the Mass text is recited. Ideally the hymn or the antiphon should be sung/recited by the entire assembly; if this is not possible, it may be sung/recited by the choir or by a reader or by one of the faithful. Otherwise it is said by the celebrant after his greeting or introduction, as noted on page 6. The entrance hymn serves "to open the celebration, encourage the unity of the assembly and lead them spiritually into the mystery of the liturgical season or feast being celebrated"[5].

When the ministers are vested, the celebrant puts incense into the censer (if incense is used) and the procession begins. All who walk in the procession keep the hands joined unless carrying something.

Upon reaching the sanctuary the crossbearer places the crucifix in its base in front of the altar, or elsewhere if a crucifix is already there. The servers carrying candles place them on the credence table unless they are to be used for the Mass near the altar, and go to their seats. Neither they nor the crossbearer make any reverence on entering the sanctuary; rather they should do so when the celebrant makes his reverence and in the same manner as he does — a profound bow or a genuflection.

---

[4] See Use of Incense in appendix, n. 3.
[5] Cfr. Gen. Instr., n. 25.

Others in the procession make the proper reverence upon entering the sanctuary and go to their places. The lectionary or the Book of Gospels, if it is borne in the procession, is taken directly to its proper place: the lectionary to the ambo, the Book of Gospels to the mensa at the center of the altar. The celebrant makes the proper reverence — a profound bow or a genuflection if the tabernacle is nearby- and with the deacon kisses the altar as a mark of veneration[6].

If incense is used at this time[7], the thurifer presents the censer. The incense, if blessed in the sacristy, need not be blessed again. The celebrant incenses the altar, saying nothing. He walks slowly, to his right, around the altar. If the crucifix is on the altar or in front of the altar, it is incensed first; otherwise it is incensed when the celebrant is opposite it as he circles the altar. No bow is called for before, during or after the incensing, and no one is incensed at this time.

After the incensing or, if this is not done, after kissing the altar, the celebrant goes directly to the chair where he remains until after the prayer of the faithful, departing from it only (and if need be) to give the homily. All the ministers are standing.

When the entrance hymn or the antiphon is ended, the celebrant blesses himself and says aloud: IN THE NAME OF THE FATHER, AND OF THE SON. . . . The ministers and the people bless

---

[6] It is the whole altar, symbol of Christ and center of the Eucharistic assembly, that is venerated here and not just the relics enclosed therein.

[7] The use of incense at this time makes the worship more solemn and it is a sign of prayer rising to God.

themselves but say only the response: AMEN.

The server brings the sacramentary before the celebrant, if need be, and holds it for him.

The celebrant, in recognition of the presence of Christ in His Church and in the assembly, greets the people, extending the hands and saying one of the given formulas. The people make the appropriate response. "By this greeting and the response of the people, the mystery of the Church in assembly is manifested"[8]. The celebrant's manner of greeting should be warm and friendly and evidence his faith in and awareness of the sacred character and the awesome mystery of the Eucharistic celebration.

Now the priest, or a qualified minister, may give the people a brief introduction to the liturgical mystery being celebrated; it should not, however, anticipate the Liturgy of the Word — hence it should be well-prepared.

If there was no entrance hymn or the people or a minister did not recite the antiphon, the priest himself now reads the given antiphon, or he may include it in the brief introduction.

Then follows the penitential rite or, if it is a Sunday, the blessing and sprinkling of holy water may take place.

THE PENITENTIAL RITE. The celebrant, with the hands joined, invites the assembly to a spirit of repentance before celebrating the Eucharist. He uses the given formula[9], or another of his

---

[8] Gen. Instr., n. 28.
[9] 'Brethren' or 'Friends', and the like, may be used in place of 'Brothers and sisters'.

The server ministers the Sacramentary during the introductory rites.

own composition[10]. A period of silent reflection follows. Then he continues, selecting one of the given formulas of the penitential act. The priest does well who alternates these formulas, thus allowing the faithful to become familiar with all three.

In Form A the celebrant and the people recite together the simplified *CONFITEOR*, striking the breast once at the words: . . . THROUGH MY OWN FAULT. . . . Form B is a short dialogue between the celebrant and the people, as indicated. In Form C the series of invocations is led by the priest or the deacon or the lector, and after each one the pepole respond: LORD, HAVE MERCY. The invocations and the responses may be sung. In Form C the given invocations may be replaced by others more suited to the occasion.

The celebrant always concludes the penitential rite (whichever Form is used) with the petition: MAY ALMIGHTY GOD HAVE MERCY. . . .[11]. The people respond: AMEN.

THE *KYRIE*, or short litany of acclamations-invocations to Christ the Lord, is sung or recited, but if Form C of the penitential rite was used, the *Kyrie* is omitted — to avoid duplication. Now these invocations are not a priestly function, hence they should be led by one of the ministers or, if sung, by the choir or the cantor. If no suitable minister does so, or the choir does not sing them, the invocations are said by the priest and the peo-

---

[10] Cfr. Appendix, n. 36.
[11] The faithful should be reminded occasionally that the penitential rite does not include Sacramental Absolution from serious sin.

ple respond by repeating the same words. Thus each invocation is said twice; but, if sung, they may be repeated more often.

Then the *GLORIA*, if it is to be added, is sung or recited.

THE BLESSING AND SPRINKLING HOLY WATER. This ceremony is optional; it may be added at all Masses with a congregation on all Sundays, including the anticipated Mass on Saturday evenings. It may be added in all churches and oratories. It should be kept in mind that when the asperges ceremony takes place, both the penitential rite and the *KYRIE* are omitted.

A server brings before the celebrant the vessel of water to be blessed and the container of salt, if used. The priest, with hands joined, invites the people to pray, singing or saying the given formula, or another of his own composition. After a silent pause the priest, with hands joined, blesses the water saying one of the given formulas (a special formula is said during Eastertide). The priest then blesses the salt, if used, saying the given formula and pours some into the water. The people respond: AMEN.

Taking the aspergill and dipping it into the newly blessed water the celebrant blesses himself, the ministers and the clergy present; then he blesses the people. He should do this passing through the church with a server accompanying him and carrying the blessed water. If this is not convenient, he may bless the people from the chair or from the edge of the sanctuary. An appropriate hymn or

---

[12] Cfr. Newsletter, Sept.-Oct. 1972, p. 4.

antiphon should be sung during the blessing.

When he returns to the chair and the hymn is ended, the priest, with hands joined, sings or says the concluding prayer, without prefacing it with the words: Let us pray. The people respond: AMEN.

Then the Gloria, if it is to be added, is sung or recited.

THE *GLORIA*, the hymn by which "the Church, assembled in the Holy Spirit, glorifies God the Father and the Lamb, and makes supplication to him"[13], is sung or recited on all Sundays outside of Advent and Lent, on liturgical days of the rank of Solemnity or Feast, and at other particularly solemn local celebrations. It is added also on the days within the octaves of Christmas and Easter.

Ideally the *GLORIA* should be sung or recited by the whole assembly. It is not necessary for the celebrant to intone the *GLORIA;* he may do so or the leader of song or the commentator may begin it.

At a funeral, when the casket is received by the priest at the door of the church just prior to the Mass, the greeting is not repeated at the chair, and the penitential rite/*Kyrie* are omitted. After the priest kisses the altar at the beginning, he goes to the chair and sings/says the opening prayer[14].

THE OPENING PRAYER. The celebrant, with hands joined, invites the people to pray. He may do this in the usual way, saying: LET US PRAY and adding the expanded invitation given in the

---

[13] Gen. Instr., n. 31.
[14] Newsletter, Apr-May 1971, p. 3.

sacramentary or, if he so wish, he may make it more concrete and effective by using his own words.

After a short silence to allow the assembly to recall that they are in the presence of God and to formulate their own intentions in their hearts, the celebrant extends the hands and proclaims the opening prayer[15]. The conclusion of the prayer is an integral part of the opening prayer and it should be said with the same care that is required for the rest of the prayer. The people make the prayer their own by responding: AMEN.

The opening prayer is the first of the 'presidential prayers'; the others being: the prayer over the gifts, the Eucharistic prayer and the prayer after Communion. It is the exclusive role of the priest "who presides over the assembly in the person of Christ, to address these prayers to God in the name of the holy people in its entirely and of all those present"[16]. He should voice these prayers loudly and distinctly[17].

There is only one prayer said at this point of the Mass and it always ends with the long conclusion; the prayer over the gifts and the prayer after communion have the short conclusion.

The server who has been holding the sacramentary before the celebrant now closes it and places it on the credence table. It will not be used again until the preparation of the gifts at the altar. All in the church sit.

---
[15] The former rubric calling for the people to kneel at the Collect in Lenten weekday Masses has been deleted from the Missal. Cfr. Gen. Instr., Apr-May, 1970, p. 8 (n. 21) and Id. Dec. 1969, p. 1, n. 1).

[16] Gen. Instr., n. 10.

[17] Gen. Instr., n. 12.

It will be well for all priests to familiarize themselves with detailed rubrics of the Missal governing the choice of Mass formularies and of their several parts. The principal rubrics of frequent concern on the choice of the Mass formulary are:

1. On Sundays, weekdays of Advent, the Christmas season, Lent and the Easter season, on solemnities, feasts and obligatory memorials, the Mass with a congregation follows the calendar of the church where the celebration takes place.

2. On optional memorials occurring on the weekdays of Lent, Advent before December 17, on the weekdays of Christmas and Easter seasons, the priest may choose the weekday Mass, the Mass of the Saint or of one of the Saints whose memorial is observed, or the Mass of a Saint listed in the martyrology that day.

3. On optional memorials occurring on weekdays of Lent, of Advent from Dec. 17 to Dec. 24, during the octave of Christmas and on the weekdays of Lent, except Ash Wednesday and Holy Week, the priest celebrates the Mass of the day, but he may take the opening prayer from a memorial listed in the Ordo for that day.

4. On optional memorials in ordinary time, the priest may choose the weekday Mass, the Mass of the memorial, the Mass of a Saint listed in the martyrology for that day, a Mass for various occasions, or a votive Mass.

These and other directives are found in the General Instruction on the Roman Missal,nn. 313-324 and 326-341; also at the beginning of the Sanctoral proper, of the Commons, of the Masses and Prayers *ad diversa*, and of Masses for the dead.

The appropriate ritual provides directives for the use of Ritual Masses.

# LITURGY OF THE WORD
## General Principles

"The readings from Sacred Scripture together with the chants between them constitute the principal part of the Liturgy of the Word, and the homily, the profession of faith and the universal prayer develop and conclude it"[18]. "In the readings the Table of God's Word is provided for the faithful and the treasures of the Bible are laid open for them"[19].

The Scripture readings are proclaimed from the ambo, even when the celebrant, in the absence of other ministers, does so. If there is no ambo (as may be the case in a small chapel,), they are read at some other suitable place.

The readings at Mass must be chosen exclusively from those contained in the lectionary mandated by the U.S. Bishops on Nov. 1, 1971. No other readings whatsoever may be used. The Sacred Congregation for Divine Worship ruled on this matter in its Third Instruction (Sept. 5, 1970): "Full importance must be given to the Liturgy of the Word in the Mass. Other readings, whether from sacred or profane authors of past or present may never be substituted for the Word of God" (n. 2, a).

It will be well for all priests to familiarize themselves with the norms governing the choice of texts

---

[18] Gen. Instr., n. 33.
[19] Gen. Instr., n. 34.

for the readings found in the Introduction to the lectionary, Ch. 1, n. VII. For Ritual Masses, during which certain sacraments and sacramentals are celebrated, a wide selection of texts is found in the lectionary. The pastoral needs of the participating group should guide the priest in making his choice of readings.

"The pattern of three readings for Sundays and solemnities, in accord with the *Ordo Lectionum*, should be completely implemented"[20]; on liturgical days of lesser rank one reading precedes the Gospel.

When at the *ambo* the lector, or other minister, should proclaim the readings from the lectionary and not from a missalette or other participation pamphlet[21].

The proclamation of the biblical readings is a ministerial function and should be done by a minister other than the celebrant. The first reading (and the second, if there are three) is read by the lector or, in his absence, by the deacon; the Gospel is read by the deacon or by another priest or, if none is available, by the celebrant[22]. Only when there is neither a deacon nor another priest does the celebrant himself read all the readings.

To allow for wider participation of ministers, individual lectors may be assigned to each reading before the Gospel. The lector has his own proper function in the Eucharistic celebration which he himself should perform even when ministers of high-

---

[20] Newsletter, Dec. 1969, p. 2, n. 6.
[21] Newsletter, May 1974, pp. 3-4.
[22] The celebrant should not read the Gospel if another priest or deacon is present to do so. (Newsletter, Sept-Oct. 1971, p. 3).

er order are present[23]. He should be well prepared for his role[24].

When brief comments on a particular reading before its proclamation are made by the lector, they should be concise and well-prepared. The lector may pause after each reading to allow for silent reflection. He concludes each reading with the words: THIS IS THE WORD OF THE LORD, and the people respond: THANKS BE TO GOD.

The homily, if given by the celebrant, may be preached either at the ambo or at the chair; if by another, at the ambo.

The profession of faith and the prayer of the faithful are led by the celebrant standing at the chair. In the prayer of the faithful the celebrant says the introduction and the concluding prayer from the chair, and the deacon or commentator reads the intentions from the *ambo*.

## The Ceremonies

When the people have made their response after the opening prayer of the Mass, the celebrant sits at the chair. If he so wishes, he may briefly introduce the Liturgy of the Word before seating himself[25].

The assigned lector goes to the ambo and proclaims the reading. If he passes before the taber-

---

[23] A list of aids for preparing lectors is found in Newsletter, Jul-Aug. 1971, p. 8).

[24] Gen. Instr., n. 66, revised 12/23/72, reads: "The lector is instituted for the proclamation of the readings from Sacred Scriptures, except the Gospel. He may also announce the intentions of the general intercessions and, in the absence of a cantor of psalm, sing the psalm between the readings".

[25] See appendix, n. 36.

nacle on his way, he genuflects towards it. After the first reading and the people's acclamation, he sits at his place, unless it is his duty also to lead the psalm.

If there is a psalmist (ideally he should be distinct from the lector[26]), he comes to the lectern (the one used by the commentator) to sing or say the responsorial psalm. If need be, he may do this from the ambo.

The responsorial psalm, "which is an integral part of the Liturgy of the Word"[27], is sung or recited after the first reading. The people participate in it by means of the refrain or response, unless the psalm is sung straight through. If it is not sung, it must be recited — for the responsorial psalm may not be omitted.

If a second reading is to be read before the Gospel, the assigned lector goes to the ambo to proclaim it. At its end he adds: THIS IS THE WORD OF THE LORD, as at the first reading; the people respond: THANKS BE TO GOD.

On the solemnities of Easter Sunday and Pentecost Sunday the sequence must be sung or recited before the *ALLELUIA*. It may be sung by the choir or by the psalmist or other; or it is recited by the assembly or by the lector. The other sequences are optional.

After the second reading or, if only one, after the responsorial psalm (or after the sequence, when added), all stand and the ALLELUIA is sung. Its purpose is to acclaim the proclamation of the Gospel. The double or triple *ALLELUIA* is sung

---

[26] Newsletter, Apr-May, 1971, p. 7, Replies to Questions.
[27] Cfr. Gen. Instr., n. 36.

The proclamation of the Gospel.

by the cantor or the choir, and it may be repeated by people; the cantor or the choir sings the given verse and the people repeat the *ALLELUIA*. The *ALLELUIA* of the Gospel should be sung; if this is impossible, it should be omitted[28].

During Lent the *Alleluia* is replaced by another chant as indicated in the lectionary[29].

If incense is used at the Gospel, it is prepared during the singing of the *Alleluia;* the celebrant is standing. The thurifer brings the censer and boat to the chair where the priest puts incense into the censer and blesses it with the simple sign of the cross, saying nothing. At the same time the two servers with their candles stand by the thurifer before the celebrant's chair, if space allows. When the deacon has received the blessing, they precede him to the *ambo*. There the servers stand on either side of the *ambo* and the thurifer stands where he can easily give the censer to the deacon.

When the Book of Gospels is used it should be on the altar from the start of the Mass. The deacon, standing before the celebrant and making a profound bow, asks the blessing in a low voice: FATHER, GIVE ME YOUR BLESSING. The celebrant, in a low voice, blesses the deacon saying: THE LORD BE IN YOUR HEART . . . ., and makes the sign of the cross over him. The deacon responds: AMEN, goes to the altar and takes the Book of Gospels with both hands and, holding it upright, follows the candlebearers to the *ambo*. He opens the Book to the Gospel text and, with

---

[28] Newsletter, Apr., 1973, p. 3.
[29] Under Lenten Season or n. 224.

hands joined, greets the people, saying: THE LORD BE WITH YOU and pauses for their response. He identifies the reading and makes a small sign of the cross with his thumb on the text and then on his forehead, lips and breast. After the people's response he incenses the Book, or, if incense is not used, with hands joined he proceeds to proclaim the Gospel.

After the Gospel has been read the deacon says: THIS IS THE GOSPEL OF THE LORD. He may pause for a moment of silent reflection. While the people make their response: PRAISE TO YOU, LORD JESUS CHRIST, he kisses the text, raising the book somewhat in doing so and saying inaudibly: MAY THE WORDS OF THE GOSPEL WIPE AWAY OUR SINS. He then returns to his place; the Book remains at the ambo. The servers who held the candles at the Gospel place them on the credence table and go to their places. Neither the celebrant nor the deacon is incensed.

In the absence of a deacon another priest[30] should read the Gospel from the lectionary already at the ambo. The priest does not ask the celebrant's blessing (even if the Ordinary is presiding), but he goes before the altar, makes a profound bow and prays: ALMIGHTY GOD, CLEANSE MY HEART . . . (*Munda cor meum* . . ). Then he goes to the *ambo* and with hands joined proclaims the Gospel and concludes it in the same manner as

---

[30] The 'Other Priest' (and the deacon) referred to here is one who exercises his office during the whole of the Mass — hence will wear the liturgical vesture proper to his order — alb, stole hanging down in front, for the priest; alb, stole worn diagonally (and the dalmatic) for the deacon.

would the deacon.

Much of the time the celebrant himself must read the Gospel in the absence of a deacon or another priest. In this case he goes before the altar at the end of the *Alleluia*, makes a profound bow and prays: ALMIGHTY GOD, CLEANSE MY HEART . . . .; he then goes to the *ambo* and proceeds as would the deacon. If he uses incense, he blesses it as above at the chair during the *Alleluia*, and the thurifer precedes him to the altar and then to the ambo. Servers with their candles, as described above, may accompany the reading of the Gospel. After the greeting and the identification of the text, he incenses the book. He is not incensed after the reading.

In the absence of both the deacon and the lector the celebrant himself reads all the readings. After the opening prayer of the Mass he goes to the ambo, where he proclaims the Scripture lessons, leads the responsorial psalm and sings the *Alleluia*/verse, unless the choir or the people do so. If he uses incense, he prepares it at the ambo during or after the Alleluia. Then the celebrant makes a profound bow and says the prayer: ALMIGHTY GOD . . . . , greets the people and identifies the text. Then he takes the censer in hand and incenses the book. He proclaims the Gospel and concludes it as would the deacon. The celebrant is not incensed at this time.

The two servers with candles may take their places at the side of the ambo when the thurifer brings the censer — during the *Alleluia*.

After the Scripture readings the celebrant (or the deacon or another priest) gives the homily. Ideally the celebrant himself should do so, and he may stand either at the chair or at the ambo to give the homily.

"The purpose of the homily is to explain the readings and make them relevant for the present day. This is the task of the priest, and the faithful should not add comments or engage in dialogue during the homily"[31].

The homily should never be omitted in Masses with a congregation on Sundays and on Holy Days — ". . . it is necessary for the nourishment of the Christian life"[32]. The homily is called for also at nuptial and funeral Masses[33]. It is warmly recommended on the weekdays of Advent, Lent and Easter[34]; it may be included on other weekdays as well[34]. The sign of the cross is not made before or after the homily.

A period of silent reflection on the Word of God, during which all sit, may be observed after the homily.

After the silence or after the homily all stand to say the Profession of Faith (the Nicene Creed). The Profession of Faith is required on all Sundays and solemnities; it may be added at other solemn local celebrations. It is said by the entire assembly and, even if sung, the people shoul take part in it, singing it throughout or in alternating fashion with the choir. The Profession of Faith need not be intoned by the celebrant.

---

[31] Third Instr., n. 2,a; and Newsletter, Nov. 1970, p. 7, n. 2.
[32] Gen. Instr., n. 41.
[33] Rite of Marriage, n. 22; Rite of Funerals, n. 41.
[34] Cfr. Gen. Instr., n. 42.

A profound bow should be made by all at the words: BY THE POWER OF THE HOLY SPIRIT . . . BECAME MAN. All too frequently this bow is overlooked; the faithful should be reminded of it from time to time, and they will observe it if they see the celebrant and the ministers doing so. On two days a genuflection is made rather than the bow at these same words: on the solemnities of Annunciation and of Christmas.

Normally the celebrant presides over the Profession of Faith while standing at the chair.

After the Profession of Faith or, if this was not said, after the homily, the celebrant, still standing at the chair, presides over the prayer of the faithful[35].

Without saying LET US PRAY, the celebrant says aloud the invitation, using the given words or formulating his own. The deacon, or the lector or another minister, stands at the lectern or at the ambo to read the list of intentions, after each of which the entire congregation voices an invocation or observes a moment of silence.

The celebrant, at the chair, says the concluding prayer. The celebrant may moderate the prayer of the faithful at the ambo[36], which may be preferable when he himself voices the intentions, in the absence of the deacon or other minister.

The prayer of the faithful is normally included

---

[35] An excellent discussion of the universal prayer is found in Newsletter, Sept-Oct. 1970, p. 7. This prayer at nuptial Masses is said BEFORE the Profession of Faith, when this is added. (Rite of Marriage, n. 29).

[36] Cfr. Gen. Instr., n. 99.

"in every form of the Mass"[37], even in a Mass without a congregation[38]. It may be said or sung.

The prayer of the faithful concludes the Liturgy of the Word; all sit while the ministers prepare the altar for the Liturgy of the Eucharist.

# LITURGY OF THE EUCHARIST
## Preparation of the Gifts

After the general intercessions (prayer of the faithful), the ministers prepare the altar, while the celebrant remains seated at the chair. Now the proper ministers for this function are, in order of preference, the deacon who is assisted by the servers, the acolyte with the assistance of the servers, or the servers themselves. They put the sacramentary and stand in its place, unfold and spread the corporal at the center and carry to the altar the chalice (without the veil) with the purificator and place it at the right end of the mensa.

If the paten holding the large host and the ciborium, or the larger paten holding the large host and smaller ones, are not to be brought forward in the procession of the faithful, the ministers will bring them to the altar when they bring the chalice.

The chalice veil, which may be either always white or the color of the vestments, is folded by the server and left on the credence table.

When, for lack of suitable ministers, the chalice must be on the altar from the start of the Mass, it should stand, covered with the veil, at the right

---
[37] Cfr. Gen. Instr., n. 15.
[38] Cfr. Gen. Instr., n. 220.

The preparation of the gifts of bread and wine.

end of the mensa (not at the center) or at its side. In any case, the corporal is not unfolded and spread at the center until this point in the celebration.

The procession of gifts is highly recommended as a visible sign of the participation of the congregation in the sacrifice. It may be had at any Mass; but is especially fitting on Sundays, Holy Days, and on other occasions of special importance to the people.

In the procession the altarbreads to be used at Mass and the cruets of water and wine are brought forward by selected members of the faithful. Weekly contributions and other things for use in the church (such as candles, incense, and gifts of the parishioners to the church, etc.), as well as gifts for the poor brought by the people and collected in the church, may also be brought forward in this procession, but these are put in a place near the Eucharistic table. It is most fitting to allow families and individuals who donate a new vestment, a lectionary or sacramentary or the like, to the parish to bring these gifts and present them in the offertory procession.

It will involve the congregation more if the people who bring forward the gifts are varied rather than always being the same group.

This procession is neither the time nor the occasion for demonstrations of any kind; hence banners and signs of any sort should be excluded in Masses of the community.

While the ministers prepare the altar the offertory procession of the faithful is formed at the rear of the church and it moves forward slowly when the celebrant is ready to accept the gifts. Singing or instrumental music may accompany the procession, or it is done in silence. The singing and/or music must end in time for the celebrant to invite the people to pray (before PRAY, BRETHREN ..) just before the prayer over the gifts, which concludes the preparatory rite and leads into the Eucharistic prayer itself[39].

When the procession of the faithful bearing the gifts is formed, the celebrant goes with his ministers to the edge of the sanctuary to accept the gifts which, in turn, he hands to the servers to be taken to their proper place. When there is no procession, after the ministers have readied the altar, the celebrant goes to the altar for the preparation of the gifts.

It must be kept in mind that this a 'preparatory' rather than an 'offertory' rite, as we knew it before. The prescribed formulas in the new sacramentary which accompany the placing of the sacrificial elements on the altar, do make mention of 'offering', but in the sense of 'presenting' or 'designating', and not in the sense of 'oblation'. The priest, in his gestures, should exercise care not to give the old notion of offering.

When the chalice with the paten has been on the altar from the start of the Mass (as noted on p. 25), the celebrant first uncovers it, spreads the corporal at the center, and then proceeds to prepare the sacrificial elements.

The celebrant (or the deacon) places the ciborium on the corporal and removes the cover. The celebrant takes the paten with the host on it and,

---

[39] Cfr. Gen. Instr., n. 50.

holding it with both hands only slightly (*aliquantulum*) above the corporal, says the prayer of blessing: BLESSED ARE YOU . . . then he rests the paten with the host on it on the corporal. If there is no singing at this time, he MAY say the prayer aloud, thus allowing the faithful to respond with their acclamation: BLESSED BE GOD . . . This holds true also of the prayer of blessing with the chalice. The ciborium may remain open or uncovered on the altar.

The use of the larger paten, capable of holding the altarbreads for the celebrant, ministers and at least some of the faithful, is commendable[40].

The celebrant then, with hands joined, moves to the right end of the altar to prepare the chalice, unless it was done before the Mass or unless the deacon will do this function. The pouring of wine and water into the chalice is done away from the center of the altar. It may even be done by the deacon at the credence table just before he brings the chalice to the altar. The ministers bring the cruets to the side of the altar and present them as needed.

The celebrant pours the wine into the chalice and then a little water[41], saying the prescribed prayer. When a deacon assists, he pours both the wine and the water into the chalice, saying the prescribed prayer, and then hands the chalice to the celebrant.

Standing at the center the celebrant takes the

---

[40] Cfr. Gen. Instr., nn. 293 and 56,h.

[41] No mention is made in the Missal of the need to wipe drops of wine/water from inside of the cup. Neither is it banned, however.

chalice with both hands and holds it slightly above the corporal, saying the prayer of blessing: BLESSED ARE YOU . . . . As with the paten, he MAY say this prayer aloud. The use of the pall is now optional[42]. Then, bowing low, he prays: LORD GOD. . . . .

Incense may be used at this point[43]. In which case the thurifer presents the censer and the celebrant, standing at the center, puts incense into it and blesses it with a simple sign of the cross, saying nothing. The celebrant takes the censer in hand and incenses the gifts with the usual three double swings, as when incensing other things. The multiple circles and crosses formerly prescribed have been discontinued. He MAY incense also the crucifix and the altar. At a funeral Mass the priest, if he uses incense at this point, may also incense the casket[44].

Then the deacon or another minister may incense the celebrant and the congregation[45].

Then or, if incense was not used, after the prayer: LORD GOD . . . , the celebrant again moves to the right end of the altar to wash his hands[46], and, while doing so, says: LORD, WASH AWAY. . . . A server holds the basin or dish and pours the water over the priest's hands, while another presents the towel for drying the hands.

Or, if preferred, a bowl filled with water is held by the minister and the priest dips his hands into

---

[42] Cfr. Gen. Instr., n. 80,c.
[43] See appendix, Use of Incense. No. 3.
[44] Rite of Funerals, n. 3.
[45] Cfr. Gen. Instr., n. 51.
[46] Cfr. *Notitiae,* 1970, p. 38, n. 27.

it and dries them.[47] The celebrant returns to the center with hands joined.

Turning to face the people, if need be, the celebrant slowly extends and rejoins the hands as he invites them to prayer, saying aloud: PRAY, BRETHREN. . . . If a hymn is being sung at this time, he should wait until it is ended before voicing the invitation to pray. With the hands joined, he should allow the people to complete their response before looking in the sacramentary for the prayer over the gifts.

The purpose of this invitation is to stimulate a religious atmosphere and a real sense of profound prayer in the faithful that will enable them to enter fully into the Eucharistic prayer.

Then the celebrant extends his hands and sings or says the prayer over the gifts. For the conclusion of the prayer he rejoins his hands. The people respond: AMEN. The short conclusion is always used.

# THE EUCHARISTIC PRAYER[48]

The Eucharistic prayer, which begins with the dialogue into the preface and ends with the doxology, is the central part of the entire celebration. The whole prayer is one of thanksgiving, praise and sanctification.[49]

The Eucharistic prayer is the most important of the presidential prayers and its proclamation is re-

---

[47] The *Lavabo* is an expression of the priest's desire for inward purification. It may not be omitted. Cfr. Gen. Instr., n. 52.

[48] See appendix, n. 13, 18, 33-35.

[49] Cfr. Gen. Instr., n. 54.

served to the celebrant. Through the responses and acclamations the faithful express their acceptance and ratification of what the celebrant says on their behalf and unite themselves in heart and mind with Christ in whose name the celebrant presides.

The celebrant may make a few remarks by way of exhortation on the basic theme of the particular preface being used before beginning it[50]. However, caution is the word here lest excessive verbiage on the part of the celebrant taint the celebration. The content of this brief exhortation may easily be drawn from the heading to each preface in the sacramentary. The priest should refrain from making additional comments during the Eucharistic prayer. A short pause before saying: THE LORD BE WITH YOU is a useful psychological break and allows attention to be re-focused when this central prayer of the Mass begins.

When the priest says a prayer, especially the Eucharistic prayer, he must avoid not only a dry, monotonous style of delivery, but also an overly subjective and emotional way of speaking and acting. As the one presiding over the celebration, he must be very careful in reading and singing to help those taking part to form a true community, as they celebrate and live the memorial of the Lord[51].

At the Mass of the parish community none of the faithful should be invited to stand around the altar, inside the sanctuary, during the Liturgy of the Eucharist. Civil authorities attending the Mass

---

[50] Cfr. Third Instruction, n. 3,f; also see appendix, nn. 34 and 36.

[51] Cfr. Eucharistic Prayers, Letter to Presidents . . . . , n. 17.

should have a place in the body of the church.[52]

In beginning the introductory dialogue of the preface the celebrant's voice should be fresh and vigorous to give impetus to the prayer that follows.

The large host to be consecrated during the Eucharistic prayer must remain unbroken until time for Communion[53]. After the consecration the celebrant need not (though he may) join the thumbs and forefingers; if there is any fragment of the Host on his fingers, he purifies his fingers over the paten. During the ablutions after Communion, the priest purifies and dries his fingers only "if need be"[54].

A great variety of new prefaces is found in the sacramentary and this affords the celebrant a valuable means of keeping the different aspects of the mystery of salvation before the minds of the faithful[55]. It should be utilized to its full potential. Let the celebrant carefully note the rubric that accompanies each of the new prefaces and indicates when

---

[52] The sanctuary is the place for the ministers and should be set off from the body of the church, which is the place for the faithful. (Cfr. Gen. Instr., nn. 258 and 273).

[53] It is an abuse, which evidences a misunderstanding of the structure of the Eucharistic celebration, for the priest to break the host when he says, in the words of the institution,: ". . . He broke the bread . . . ". The General Instruction (n. 55,d) reminds the celebrant that ". . . in the words and actions of Christ, the sacrifice He instituted at the Last Supper is celebrated . . .". The bread is broken for Communion, as it was by Christ Himself, AFTER the thanksgiving. The prayer of thanksgiving in the Mass embraces the whole of the Eucharistic prayer, from the introductory dialogue of the preface to the final doxology inclusively. (See *Notitiae* 1973, p. 320, footnote).

[54] Cfr. Second Instruction (Mar. 4, 1967), n. 12.

[55] Cfr. Gen. Instr., n. 321.

its use is required or permitted.

Special prefaces are provided for some ritual Masses, such as: Marriage, Religious Profession; for some of the Commons, such as: Dedication of a church, an altar; and for certain civil holidays, such as: Independence Day and Thanksgiving Day. When a strictly proper preface is given for any celebration, it should be used; otherwise one of the current seasonal prefaces (Lent, Easter, Ordinary Time) or one of the common prefaces[56].

Only approved texts of the prefaces found in the sacramentary or in the Ritual Books, approved by the National Conference of Catholic Bishops and confirmed by the Holy See, may be used at Mass. No other texts may be used.

Since the National Conference of Catholic Bishops[57] has called for the faithful to kneel from after the HOLY, HOLY, HOLY . . . until after the AMEN of the doxology, the celebrant would do well to pause a few seconds before continuing the Eucharistic prayer, to allow the people to kneel. Thus the priest's opening words will not be drowned out by the rattle of kneelers.

To begin the preface the priest extends his hands and says or sings: THE LORD BE WITH YOU; he raises the extended hands when he says or sings: LIFT UP YOUR HEART; he keeps the hands raised and extended when he says or sings: LET US GIVE THANKS . . . The priest does not join his hands at the people's responses, but keeps them extended until the HOLY, HOLY, HOLY . . .

---

[56] Eucharistic prayers II and IV have their own prefaces. Cfr. Gen. Instr., n. 322.

[57] See Newsletter, Apr.-May 1970, p. 8.

The priest shows the Host (and then the chalice with the Precious Blood) to the faithful.

These gestures, as well as others during the Mass, should be natural and serve to express the content of the words they accompany. At the end of the preface, he rejoins his hands and sings or says, in unison with the congregation, the HOLY, HOLY, HOLY . . .

With the hands extended, the celebrant alone continues the Eucharistic prayer.[58]

Since the gestures which accompany the Consecration and the doxology are common to all four Eucharistic prayers, they are described here but once to avoid repetition.

## The Words of Institution or Consecration

At the place indicated in the Eucharistic prayer he uses, the celebrant bows slightly and, holding the large host with both hands a little above the paten, says or sings: TAKE THIS, ALL OF YOU, AND EAT IT. Reverently and distinctly he then pronounces the words of consecration of the bread. Standing erect, he then shows the consecrated Host to the faithful for their adoration before resting It on the paten. Then he genuflects in adoration.[59]

As he says the words: WHEN SUPPER WAS ENDED HE TOOK THE CUP, the celebrant takes the chalice (removing the pall, if used) with both hands and, holding it a little above the corporal, continues: AGAIN HE HAVE THANKS AND

---

[58] Newsletter, Apr.-May 1970, p. 8, n. 21.

[59] The genuflection is a gesture of adoration and should be seen as such. It ought to be calm and crisp, and certainly not a bob or a sleepy effort in which the altar becomes merely a convenient prop for the celebrant's weight. (*Sounds Effective,* by Raymond Clarke, p. 69. Chapman).

PRAISE, GAVE THE CUP TO HIS DISCIPLES, AND SAID. He bows slightly and says or sings: TAKE THIS, ALL OF YOU, AND DRINK FROM IT. Reverently and distinctly he then pronounces the words of Consecration of the wine. Standing erect, he then shows the chalice with the Precious Blood to the people for their adoration, as he did with the Host. He rests the chalice on the corporal (replacing the pall, if used) and genuflects in adoration. He then invites the people to proclaim the Mystery of Faith[60].

A slight variation in the wording before the Consecration of the wine occurs in Eucharistic Prayer IV. After saying: IN THE SAME WAY, HE TOOK THE CUP FILLED WITH WINE, the celebrant takes the chalice with both hands and, holding it raised above the corporal, continues: HE GAVE YOU THANKS, AND GIVING THE CUP TO HIS DISCIPLES, SAID. Bowing slightly, he says or sings: TAKE THIS, ALL OF YOU, AND DRINK FROM IT. Reverently and distinctly he then pronounces the words of Consecration of the wine. The rest is as above.

It should be noted that there is no elevation as we knew it before; rather, the celebrant raises the Host/chalice just enough above the paten/corporal to show it to the people. Certainly it should not be raised above the head of the celebrant as before.[61]

If it is deemed necessary or is desired, a server may sound the handbell a little before the Consecration (possibly at the invocation of the Holy

---

[60] Cfr. CSL, n. 28; Gen. Instr., n. 58; Newsletter, Oct.-Nov. 1969, p. 7.

[61] See appendix, n. 11.

Spirit) and again when the priest shows the Consecrated Species to the people.

## The Doxology

At the place indicated in the Eucharistic prayer he uses, the celebrant takes the chalice (removing the pall, if used) with one hand and the paten with the Host on it with the other hand and, holding them both elevated, sings or says the doxology: THROUGH HIM, WITH HIM, IN HIM. . . . . The celebrant should hold them elevated until after the people's acclamation: AMEN. The Order of Mass gives no further details of this action; hence the priest may use either hand to elevate the vessels and he may hold the chalice and paten side-by-side or the paten slightly above the chalice. If a deacon or other priest is assisting the celebrant, he raises the chalice and the celebrant the paten.

In each Eucharistic prayer the names of the Pope and of the Bishop-Ordinary of the diocese must be mentioned. By decree of the Sacred Congregation for Divine Worship (Oct. 9, 1972), mention must be made of: a) the diocesan Bishop; b) the Bishop transferred to another See who retains administration of the diocese; c) the Apostolic Administrator of the diocese provided he is a Bishop; d) the Vicar or the Prefect Apostolic. The following MAY be mentioned: a) Coadjutor or Auxiliary Bishops who assist the Ordinary in the government of the diocese; b) other ordained Bishops. When there are several, all are mentioned together after the Ordinary without mentioning their names: ". . . N., our Bishop and his assistant Bishops". No other prelate or superior may be mentioned without the permission of the Apostolic See.

Should he choose, the celebrant may sing those parts of the Eucharistic prayer which may be sung in concelebrated Masses[62]. These are, of course, in addition to the preface, the *Sanctus* and the doxology.

At this point one might recall the demand of the Sacred Congregation for Divine Worship in its Circular Letter on Eucharistic Prayers addressed to the Presidents of National Conferences of Bishops (Apr. 27, 1973) that "only those Eucharistic prayers be used which have been approved by the lawful authority of the Church, for they clearly and fully manifest the sentiments of the Church"[63].

Each one of the Eucharistic prayers is described below. The numbers attached to the quoted texts are taken from the *Ordo Missae* for easier identification.

# EUCHARISTIC PRAYER I
## *(Roman Canon)*

The celebrant, with hands extended, begins with the words: WE COME TO YOU. . . . [80], and when he says the words: THROUGH HIM WE ASK YOU TO ACCEPT AND BLESS . . . , he places the left hand on the altar while making the sign of the cross over the bread and wine. Extending his hands again, he continues the prayer. In the course of this prayer the names of the Pope and of the Ordinary are mentioned, as noted above.

---

[62] See appendix, n. 9.
[63] See appendix, n. 35.

When he pauses during the Commemoration of the Living [81] to pray for them he joins his hands. Then, with his hands extended, he continues the prayer and the one that follows it: IN UNION WITH THE WHOLE CHURCH. . . . [82]. The lines enclosed within parentheses may be omitted, and this applies throughout the Roman Canon.[64]

When a special Communicantes is prescribed, the celebrant should be careful to include it as indicated. The special Communicantes for Easter is used from the Easter Vigil Mass to the Mass of the Second Sunday of Easter inclusively.

The prayer: FATHER, ACCEPT THIS OFFERING. . . . [88] is read throughout with the hands extended. The special *HANC IGITUR* for Easter is now used from the Easter Vigil Mass to the Second Sunday of Easter inclusively. Other special *HANC IGITURs* are found in some Rituals and should be used as indicated, such as: Marriage.

With his hands outstretched over the bread and wine, the celebrant says the Invocation: BLESS AND APPROVE. . . . [90]. At the end of this prayer, he joins his hands and begins the Institution Narrative. He says the words: THE DAY BEFORE HE SUFFERED, takes the large host in his hands and, raising his eyes, continues: AND LOOKING UP TO HEAVEN . . . AND GAVE IT TO HIS DISCIPLES AND SAID. He continues the consecrations as on page 33.

After the two consecrations and the people's ac-

---

[64] If the celebrant chooses to voice the full prayer formulas, including those parts within parentheses, he should join his hands at each conclusion, as indicated in the Order of Mass.

clamation, the celebrant extends his hands and reads the Memorial: FATHER, WE CELEBRATE THE MEMORY. . . . [94], and the Offering: LOOK WITH FAVOR ON THESE OFFERINGS. . . . [95]. At the invocation: ALMIGHTY GOD, WE PRAY THAT YOUR ANGEL. . . . [96], the priest, with hands joined, bows low and says aloud the prayer through the words: . . . THE SACRED BODY AND BLOOD OF YOUR SON. Then, standing erect and signing himself with the sign of the cross, he continues: LET US BE FILLED WITH EVERY GRACE AND BLESSING.

The celebrant extends his hands again to pray the Commemoration of the Dead: REMEMBER, LORD, THOSE WHO HAVE DIED. . . . [97], but joins them during the pause indicated. The hands remain extended during the Intercessions: FOR OURSELVES, TOO, WE ASK. . . . [98]. The priest and all present strike the breast (once) at the words: THOUGH WE ARE SINNERS. The priest rejoins his hands at the conclusion: THROUGH CHRIST OUR LORD . . . . AND MAKE THEM HOLY [99].

The doxology [100] follows — as described on page 38.

# EUCHARISTIC PRAYER II

Eucharistic Prayer II has a preface of its own; but it may be used on any occasion with any preface. This Eucharistic prayer with its own preface [101] may also be used even when a seasonal preface is otherwise called for, such as: on weekdays of Adent, Lent, Eastertide or in Ordinary Time.

Understandably this does not apply on solemnities and on feasts that have their own preface (Gen. Instr., n. 322).

When the priest and the faithful together have ended the Sanctus, the celebrant, standing erect and with his hands extended, says: LORD, YOU ARE HOLY INDEED. . . . [102]. He then outstretches his hands over the bread and wine as he continues: LET YOUR SPIRIT COME . . . . . . BECOME FOR US [103]. He places his left hand on the altar while making the sign of the cross over the gifts, saying: THE BODY AND BLOOD OF OUR LORD, JESUS CHRIST. With his hands joined he continues: BEFORE HE WAS GIVEN UP TO DEATH. . . . [104]. Then he takes the host with both hands and, raising it slightly above the paten, continues: HE TOOK BREAD AND GAVE YOU THANKS. HE BROKE THE BREAD, GAVE IT TO HIS DISCIPLES, AND SAID. The priest continues the consecrations as described on page 36.

After the consecrations and the people's acclamation the celebrant extends his hands and continues the Memorial: IN MEMORY OF HIS DEATH; the Invocation: MAY ALL OF US WHO SHARE. . . . ; the Commemoration of the Dead: REMEMBER OUR BROTHERS AND SISTERS . . . . [all under 107]. In the course of these prayers, at the place indicated, the names of the Pope and of the Bishop are mentioned, as noted above on page 39. The special insert for the dead may be used any time Eucharistic Prayer II is said, whether the Mass is *Requiem*, festive or ferial. At the conclusion the celebrant rejoins his hands and says:

THROUGH YOUR SON, JESUS CHRIST.
The doxology [108] follows, as described on page 38.

# EUCHARISTIC PRAYER III

With his hands extended the celebrant says: FATHER, YOU ARE HOLY INDEED.... [109] and continues to: THE GLORY OF YOUR NAME. He outstretches his hands over the bread and wine and continues: AND SO, FATHER.... POWER OF THE HOLY SPIRIT [110]. He makes the sign of the cross over the gifts as he says: THAT THEY MAY BECOME THE BODY AND BLOOD ..... CELEBRATE THIS EUCHARIST. Joining his hands again he continues: ON THE NIGHT HE WAS BETRAYED [111]; then taking the large host with both hands, he raises it slightly above the paten and says: HE TOOK THE BREAD AND GAVE YOU THANKS ..... AND SAID. The celebrant continues the two consecrations, as described on page 37.

After the consecrations and the people's acclamation, the celebrant extends his hands and continues: FATHER, CALLING TO MIND......; the Invocations: LOOK WITH FAVOR...; the Commemorations and Petitions: GRANT THAT WE.... to: .... IN YOUR FRIENDSHIP [all under 114]. Then, joining his hands, he concludes: WE HOPE TO ENJOY....... to: ALL GOOD THINGS COME. If the celebrant so wishes he may use the special Remembrance of the Dead, as indicated in the Order of Mass. At the places indicated the names of the Saint of the day or of the patron

Saint, and the names of the Pope and of the diocesan Bishop, are mentioned.

The doxology [115] follows, as described on page 38.

# EUCHARISTIC PRAYER IV

It should be remembered that Eucharistic Prayer IV has its own preface; the two are inseparable. Hence on liturgical days or in celebrations which have their own proper preface, Eucharistic Prayer IV may not be used. However, this prayer with its inseparable preface may be used in Advent, Lent and Eastertide in Masses 'of the season', even though the seasonal preface is called for. This does not apply to any solemnity or feast that has its own proper preface (Gen. Instr., n. 322 revised).

The introductory dialogue and the preface [117] are proclaimed as described on page 36. The celebrant, with hands joined, sings or says the Sanctus with the people.

The celebrant, with hands extended, begins: FATHER, WE ACKNOWLEDGE YOUR GREATNESS . . . . TO THE FULLNESS OF GRACE [118]. The priest outstretches his hands over the bread and wine, saying: FATHER, MAY THIS HOLY SPIRIT SANCTIFY THESE OFFERINGS [119]; makes the sign of the cross over the gifts, saying: LET THEM BECOME THE BODY AND BLOOD OF JESUS CHRIST OUR LORD, and with hands joined continues: AS WE CELEBRATE THE GREAT MYSTERY WHICH HE LEFT US AS AN EVERLASTING COVENANT. In the same manner he says. HE AL-

WAYS LOVED THOSE WHO WERE HIS OWN
... to: ... WHILE THEY WERE AT SUPPER
[120]. At the words, HE TOOK BREAD. ... ,
the priest takes the large host with both hands and
holds it slightly raised above the paten. He continues the two consecrations as described on page
36, noting the variation in this Eucharistic prayer
at the consecration of the wine.

After the consecrations and the people's acclamation the celebrant extends his hands and continues
with the remainder of the prayer [123], during
which, at the places indicated, the names of the
Pope and of the diocesan Bishop are mentioned.
He rejoins the hands at the conclusion:
THROUGH WHOM YOU GIVE US EVERYTHING THAT IS GOOD.

The doxology [124] follows, as described on
page 38.

# COMMUNION RITE

When the people have concluded the great prayer of thanksgiving and its doxology with their acclamation: AMEN, the celebrant rests the chalice
and the paten on the corporal (replacing the pall,
if used).

The Communion Rite, an integral part of the
Liturgy of the Eucharist, has three parts: the preparation for Holy Communion; the distribution of
Holy Communion; the thanksgiving coupled with
the prayer after Communion.

## Preparation for Holy Communion

The celebrant, with hands joined, sings or says

the introduction to the Lord's Prayer, using either one of the given formulas or another of his own composition adapting the text ot the particular circumstances of the occasion[65].

Then, with hands extended, he sings or says with the people the OUR FATHER. After the words: DELIVER US FROM EVIL, the celebrant sings or says the embolism: DELIVER US, LORD . . . . , and, with hands joined, waits for the people to conclude it with their acclamation: FOR THE KINGDOM, THE POWER. . . . .

The prayer for peace follows. The celebrant, with hands extended, says aloud the prayer for peace: LORD, JESUS CHRIST, . . . . . OF YOUR KINGDOM; he joins his hands as he concludes the prayer: WHERE YOU LIVE FOREVER AND EVER, and waits for the people's response: AMEN. Then slowly extending and rejoining his hands the celebrant gives the peace-greeting to all the people present, singing or saying: THE PEACE OF THE LORD BE WITH YOU ALWAYS. He awaits their response: AND ALSO WITH YOU. Then the priest may add: LET US OFFER EACH OTHER THE SIGN OF PEACE (Gen. Instr., n. 112) and exchange the sign of peace with the deacon or, in his absence, with another minister, as noted in the Order of Mass, no. 129. The people exchange the sign of peace according to local custom. The celebrant should not leave his position at the altar to exchange the sign of peace with the people. (Note Appendix, n. 43)

Then the celebrant takes the Host in hand and

---

[65] See appendix, nn. 36 and 41.

breaks it over the paten (not over the chalice, as before) and drops a small portion of it into the chalice, saying: MAY THIS MINGLING......[66]. When there are several Hosts to be broken, the celebrant breaks them all at this time. During the breaking of the bread the people sing or say the invocation: LAMB OF GOD . . . , which is repeated three times. It may be repeated as often as required to accompany the action, when it is sung. In any case the last invocation always concludes with the words: GRANT US PEACE[67].

The text of this invocation never varies even in Masses for the dead. Ideally the LAMB OF GOD . . . should be sung in responsorial fashion by the choir and the people, or by the cantor and the people; it may be said in the same fashion. The celebrant does not join in saying the invocation, but he does say it in its entirety when there is none other to do so.

The rite of the breaking of the bread, even with the traditional large Host, is symbolic: it signifies that "We who are many are made into one body through communion in the one Bread of Life, which is Christ" (I Cor., 10:17). To make this significance better understood, the celebrant should wait a moment after the peace-ceremony until the faithful are again giving him their full attention.

Then the celebrant makes his own immediate preparation to receive the Body and Blood of Christ. He may choose either one or the other of the two

---

[66] If a fragment clings to his fingers, the priest cleanses the fingers over the paten. (Cfr. Gen. Instr., n. 237).

[67] Cfr. Gen. Instr., n. 56,e.

given formulas: LORD JESUS CHRIST, SON OF THE LIVING GOD . . . or: LORD JESUS CHRIST, WITH FAITH IN YOUR LOVE . . .

## Distribution of Holy Communion

When the priest has said the preparatory prayer, he genuflects. This is the third genuflection made in the Liturgy of the Eucharist; the others having been made after each of the two consecrations. He takes the Host with one hand and, holding the paten under it with the other hand, he raises it and shows it to the people (turning around, if need be) and says aloud: THIS IS THE LAMB OF GOD. . . . Then, together with the people, he says once: LORD, I AM NOT WORTHY. . . . Turning back to the altar, if need be, he prays quietly (secrete): MAY THE BODY OF CHRIST. . . . and reverently consumes the Body of Christ. No bow is called for in this action.

Pausing only long enough to swallow the host, the celebrant then takes the chalice in hand (removing the pall, if used) and says quietly: MAY THE BLOOD OF CHRIST. . . . and reverently consumes the Precious Blood. If the paten is empty at the time the priest may hold it under the chin to catch any spillage, or he may use the purificator.

Any small fragments remaining on the paten are not wiped into the chalice at this time; rather, this is done at the ablutions after the people's communion. If need be, the prest may dry his lips with the purificator. He then gives Holy Communion to the ministers and to the faithful.

It is most important that the faithful should receive the Body of the Lord in hosts consecrated at the same Mass and should share the cup, when it is permitted. Communion is thus a clearer sign of sharing in the sacrifice which is actually taking place[68].

Only a ciborium or a paten should be used in distributing Holy Communion; for Holy Communion under both kinds, drinking from the chalice is the preferred way of distribution. However, when this cannot be carried out in an orderly fashion and without any danger of irreverence towards the Precious Blood, the rite of Holy Communion under both kinds by intinction is recommended.[69]

In all churches and chapels, even of exempt religious of either sex, and, in fact, wherever Mass is legitimately celebrated outside a church or chapel, (in the United States) the consecrated Host is placed on the tongue of the communicants by the priest or the authorized minister. It may not be placed in the hand.[70]

When a deacon assists the celebrant in the distribution of Holy Communion, the deacon first receives Communion from the celebrant before taking the ciborium for the Communion of the people. When an extraordinary minister of the Eucharist[71], whether an acolyte or a designated minister, assists the celebrant in giving Holy Communion to the people, he (or she) receives Communion from the celebrant, who then hands the ciborium to the min-

---

[68] Cfr. Gen. Instr., n. 56,h.
[69] Cfr. Instruction on Sacramental Communion.
[70] See appendix, n. 42.
[71] The extraordinary minister never wears a stole: this vestment is reserved to the priest and the deacon.

ister of the Eucharist[72].

When Holy Communion from the chalice is permitted, another priest, or a deacon or an acolyte, or a designated extraordinary minister of the Eucharist must be present to administer the chalice. If the number of communicants is small, the celebrant may distribute the particles and then administer the chalice. It is not permitted that the faithful communicate by themselves or that they pass the chalice to one another[73].

During the distribution of Holy Communion a hymn may be sung, or the Communion antiphon given in the Mass text is read by the people or by a minister; otherwise it is read by the celebrant before he goes to distribute the Sacrament to the people. If there is no singing, organ or other instrumental music may be played during the Communion of the people after the appropriate antiphon has been read. The music should not be unduly loud.

Should there be no one to receive Holy Communion, the celebrant omits the words: THIS IS THE LAMB OF GOD . . . . . TO HIS SUPPER. After his preparatory prayer, the celebrant genuflects, takes the Host in his hands and says alone the words: LORD, I AM NOT WORTHY. . . . .

After the distribution of Holy Communion the deacon, or in his absence, the acolyte or the celebrant himself, collects any remaining fragments. Standing at the right side of the altar, he purifies the paten and the ciborium over the chalice, then washes the chalice and dries it with the purificator.

---

[72] See STUDY I, HOLY COMMUNION, p. 15, item a.
[73] See appendix, nn. 21-22.

This may be done at the credence table[74]. While the priest cleanses the sacred vessels, he says the prayer: GRANT, LORD, THAT WHAT WE HAVE RECEIVED . . . (*Quod ore sumpsimus . .*). A minister carries the chalice (with purificator, corporal and pall, if used) to the credence table where he covers it with the veil. If the chalice is to remain at the altar, it stands, covered with the veil, at the right end of the mensa.

When the deacon, or the acolyte[75], purifies the vessels, he may do so either at the altar or at the credence table. He omits the prayer.

The priest may wash the vessels after Mass. This is preferred, especially when there are several vessels. They are left, either at the end of the altar or at the credence table, on a corporal and covered with the veil. In this case, the priest does not say the accompanying prayer.

After he has purified the vessels or, if the deacon or acolyte does this, after the Communion of the faithful, the celebrant may go to his chair and sit for a period of silent reflection/thanksgiving, or he may do so, standing, at the center of the altar. Even with a large congregation this period of silence can be most useful as a time of peace and quiet, of private, personal prayer. A short canticle of praise or a psalm would put the crown on the silence[76].

---

[74] Cfr. Gen. Instr., nn. 120 and 138).

[75] By 'acolyte' here is meant a minister who has been installed in the Ministry of Acolyte, not a mere altarboy. (Cfr. Instr. on Sacramental Communion, Commentary, n. 4,b).

[76] The pause here, either in silence or with a hymn/psalm, meets the desire of the Bishops at the 1967 Synod that the Mass not end too abruptly after Holy Communion.

After the period of silence, the priest stands at his chair (with a server holding the sacramentary before him, if necessary) or at the center of the altar and, with hands joined, sings or says: LET US PRAY. Unless the period of silence was observed, he pauses after the invitation. Then, with the hands extended, he sings or says the prayer after Communion. He rejoins the hands for the short conclusion and waits for the people's response: AMEN.

If any liturgical service follows immediately, the prayer after Communion concludes the Mass and the dismissal is omitted (Order of Mass, n. 145).

Brief announcements by the priest or by the minister may be made at this point, but it may be better that they be made before the Introductory Rites or in the parish bulletin. A brief exhortation may be added here by the celebrant to foster an awareness on the part of the faithful of the fruits of their participation in the Mass and to urge them to carry these fruits over into their daily lives[77].

Again either at the chair or at the center of the altar, the celebrant slowly extends and rejoins the hands as he sings or says: THE LORD BE WITH YOU, to which the people respond: AND ALSO WITH YOU. Then he traces the sign of the cross over the congregation and imparts the blessing, saying: MAY ALMIGHTY GOD BLESS YOU, THE FATHER, AND THE SON, AND THE HOLY SPIRIT. The people respond: AMEN. The blessing may be sung.

---

[77] Cfr. Eucharistic Prayers, Letter to Presidents of Episcopal Conferences, Admonititions, n. 14. See Appendix, n. 36.

Then the deacon, if one assists, or the celebrant, with hands joined, dismisses the assembly with the words: GO IN PEACE TO LOVE AND SERVE THE LORD, or one of the other given formulas. The people respond: THANKS BE TO GOD.

The celebrant and the deacon, side by side, kiss the altar and, along with the other ministers, make a reverence (a profound bow or, if the tabernacle is nearby, a genuflection), and return in procession to the sacristy in the same order as they entered. When the priest chooses to remain at the chair to conclude the Mass, he and the deacon may omit kissing the altar, if it is inconvenient to do it.

## Solemn Blessings

In place of the simple blessing described above, the celebrant may, at his discretion, use another more solemn form[78], selecting the formula most appropriate to the celebration[79].

After the greeting: THE LORD BE WITH YOU and the people's response, the deacon or, in his absence, the celebrant (with hands joined) voices the invitation: BOW YOUR HEADS AND PRAY FOR GOD'S BLESSING. Another form of invitation may be used. The celebrant then extends his hands over the congregation and sings or says the three invocations, pausing after each to allow the people to respond: AMEN. After the third invocation he joins the hands and imparts the blessing indicated in the text. The people respond:

---

[78] Cfr. Gen. Instr., n. 124.

[79] The formulas for the Solemn Blessings are found in the sacramentary after the Order of Mass with a Congregation.

AMEN. The deacon or, in his absence, the celebrant dismisses the assembly as above.

The invitation, invocations and the blessings may be sung.

This more solemn blessing is a prayer addressed to the congregation, hence it should be articulated clearly and intelligently, without rushing. A momentary pause between the people's AMEN and the next portion of the prayer will help to emphasize the dignity of the blessing.

## Prayer over the People

Another option, which the celebrant may use in place of the simple or solemn form of blessing, is the Prayer over the People, formerly limited to the ferial Masses of Lent. The priest selects the prayer (any one of the 26 prayers found in the sacramentary) which most appropriately fits the celebration.

The ceremonies that accompany this prayer are the same as for the solemn blessing (above): the invitation, the prayer by the celebrant with the hands extended over the congregation, the blessing. The invitation, prayer and blessing may be sung. The dismissal follows, as above.

As with the simple blessing, the solemn form and the prayer over the people may be done either at the chair or at the center of the altar.

# Holy Communion under Both Kinds

The Roman Missal provides several methods for distributing Holy Communion under both kinds to the faithful. A server should hold the communion paten or the communicants may hold it themselves. The General Instruction describes each method in nn. 243-252.

When Communion is distributed under both kinds these preparations are made:

1. For Communion from the chalice with tubes: silver tubes for the celebrant and each communicant; a vessel of water for washing the tubes; a paten on which to place them.

2. For Communion from the chalice with a spoon, only one spoon is necessary.

3. For Communion by intinction: hosts which are neither too thin or too small, but a little thicker than usual so that when partially immersed in the Precious Blood, they may easily be given to the communicant. (Cfr. Gen. Instr., n. 243).

## Communion under Both Kinds from the Chalice

1. If there is a deacon or another priest or an acolyte:

a) The celebrant receives Communion as usual, making sure enough remains in the chalice for other communicants. He wipes the outside of the chalice with a purificator. He gives Communion to the deacon.

b) The celebrant gives the chalice and purificator to the deacon or acolyte; he himself takes the paten or ciborium with the hosts. Both go to the place for the Communion of the faithful.

c) The communicants approach, make a suitable reverence, and stand in front of the celebrant. He holds the particle slightly raised and says: THE BODY OF CHRIST. The communicant answers: AMEN and receives the Body of Christ.

d) The communicant then stands before the deacon, who says: THE BLOOD OF CHRIST. The communicant answers: AMEN, and the deacon holds out the chalice and purificator. The communicant may raise the chalice to his mouth with his own hands, taking care not to spill it. He holds the purificator under his mouth with his left hand, drinks a little from the chalice, and then returns to his place. The deacon wipes the outside of the chalice with the purificator.

e) The deacon places the chalice on the altar after all who receiving under both kinds have drunk from it. If any are present who wish to receive one kind only, the celebrant gives Communion to them and then returns to the altar. The celebrant or deacon drinks whatever remains in the chalice, and it is washed in the usual way. (Cfr. Gen. Instr., n. 244).

2. If there is no deacon, other priest, or acolyte:

a) The celebrant receives Communion as usual,

making sure enough remains in the chalice for the other communicants. He wipes the outside of the chalice with the purificator.

b) The celebrant then goes to distribute the Body of Christ as usual to all who are receiving under both kinds. The communicants approach, make a suitable reverence, and stand in front of the celebrant. After receiving the Body of Christ, they step back a little.

c) After all have received, the celebrant places the vessel on the altar and takes the chalice and purificator. The communicants again come forward and stand in front of the celebrant. He says: THE BLOOD OF CHRIST, the communicant answers: AMEN, and the celebrant holds out the chalice and purificator. The communicant holds the purificator under his mouth with his left hand, taking care that none of the Precious Blood is spilled, drinks a little from the chalice, and then returns to his place. The celebrant wipes the outside of the chalice with the purificator.

d) The celebrant places the chalice on the altar after all who are receiving under both kinds have drunk from it. If others wish to receive under one kind only, he gives the Body of Christ to them and then returns to the altar (Cfr. Gen. Instr., n. 245).

## Communion under Both Kinds by Intinction

1. If there is a deacon or another priest or an acolyte:

a) The celebrant hands the deacon the chalice and purificator and takes the paten or ciborium with the hosts. Both go to the place for distributing Holy Communion.

b) The communicants approach, make a suitable reverence, and stand in front of the celebrant. Each holds the plate under his chin while the celebrant dips a particle into the chalice and, raising it, says: THE BODY AND BLOOD OF CHRIST. The communicant responds: AMEN, receives Holy Communion, and returns to his place.

c) The Communion of those who do not receive under both kinds and the rest of the rite take place as described above. (Cfr. Gen. Instr., n. 246).

2. If there is no deacon, other priest, or acolyte:

a) After drinking some of the Precious Blood, the celebrant takes the ciborium or paten with the hosts between the index and middle fingers of his left hand and holds the chalice between the thumb and index finger of the same hand, and goes to the place for distributing Holy Communion.

b) The communicants approach, make a suitable reverence, and stand in front of the celebrant. Each holds the plate under his chin while the celebrant dips a particle into the chalice, and holds it up, saying: THE BODY AND BLOOD OF CHRIST. The communicant answers: AMEN, receives Communion and returns to his place.

c) It is also permitted to place a small table covered with a cloth and corporal at the sanctuary entrance. The celebrant places the chalice on the table in order to make distribution of Communion easier.

d) The Communion of those who do not receive under both kinds and the rest of the rite take place as described above. (Cfr. Gen. Instr., n. 247).

## Communion from the Chalice with a Tube

In this case the celebrant also uses a tube when receiving the Blood of the Lord.

If there is a deacon, or another priest, or an acolyte:

a) For the communion of the Body of Christ, everything is done as described above.

b) The communicant goes to the deacon and stands in front of him. The deacon says: THE BLOOD OF CHRIST, and the communicant responds: AMEN. He receives the tube from the minister, places it in the chalice, and drinks a little. He then removes the tube, not spilling any drops, and places it in a container of water which is held by the minister next to the deacon. Then, to cleanse the tube, he drinks a little water from it and places it in a container held by the minister.

If there is no deacon, other priest, or acolyte, the celebrant offers the chalice to each communicant in the usual way. The minister holds the container of water for cleansing the tube. (Cfr. Gen. Instr., nn. 248-249)

## Communion from the Chalice with a Spoon

If a deacon or another priest or an acolyte assists, he holds the chalice in his left hand. Each communicant holds the plate under his chin while the deacon or other priest gives him the Blood of Christ with the spoon, saying: THE BLOOD OF CHRIST. The communicant should be careful not to touch the spoon with his lips or tongue.

If there is no deacon, other priest or acolyte, the celebrant first gives the host to all who are receiving under both kinds and then gives them the Blood of the Lord. (Cfr. Gen. Instr., nn. 251-252)

Local diocesan Guidelines should be consulted to determine whether Communion from the chalice with tubes or with spoon is permitted.

The faithful should be instructed to stand to receive Holy Communion under both kinds.

# The Deacon

The deacon, whose order was held in high esteem in the early Church, has first place among the ministers. At Mass he has his own functions: he proclaims God's Word, leads the general intercessions, assists the priest, gives Communion to the faithful (in particular, ministering the chalice), and sometimes gives directions to the congregation[80].

The functions of the deacon are always the same whether he is ordained to the transitional diaconate (a cleric preparing for the priesthood) or to the permanent diaconate.

The duties assigned to the deacon may be performed by another priest, vested in alb and stole (hanging straight down in front). He may not wear the stole diagonally or the dalmatic[81].

The deacon assists the celebrant, ministering at the book or at the chalice; in the absence of lesser ministers, he carries out their duties as necessary[82]. He may accompany the celebrant as he incenses the altar.

The deacon, when exercising his office at Mass, wears the alb, the stole (hanging from the left

---

[80] Cfr. Gen. Instr., n. 61.
[81] See Newsletter, Mar. 1973, p. 3.
[82] Cfr. Gen. Instr., n. 127,c).

shoulder and fastened at the right side) and the dalmatic; he uses the amice and the cincture, if needed[83]. The stole should be the color of the priest's vestments. On less solemn occasions he may omit the dalmatic. When functioning at Mass the deacon may not wear the stole over the surplice[84].

# INTRODUCTORY RITES

When he has vested, the deacon may assist the celebrant to vest; he assists the celebrant if incense is used. If the Book of Gospels is not already on the altar, he takes it in hand and carries it to the altar, walking in front of the procession[85].

In the sanctuary the deacon makes the proper reverence to the altar, kisses it with the celebrant and goes to his chair. If he carried the Book of Gospels, he places it at the center of the mensa. If incense is used, he assists the celebrant to incense the altar, but he does not incense the priest.

At the chair the deacon blesses himself when the celebrant does so and maks all the responses, etc., with the people. He should not hold the sacramentary for the celebrant, unless there is no server available. At the blessing and sprinkling holy water, the deacon assists the celebrant and may accompany him as he blesses the congregation.

---

[83] Cfr. Gen. Instr., nn. 298-300.
[84] Cfr. Gen. Instr., n. 298.
[85] For the manner of carrying the book in procession see page 4.

# LITURGY OF THE WORD

After the opening prayer the deacon sits, unless, in the absence of the lector, he proclaims the readings.

When the cantor or the choir sings the *Alleluia* of the Gospel, the deacon, if incense is used, presents the boat. After the priest has blessed the incense or, if incense was not used, after the *Alleluia* begins, the deacon stands before the celebrant, makes a profound bow and asks the blessing: FATHER, GIVE ME YOUR BLESSING. After the blessing the deacon goes to the altar, takes the Book of Gospels with both hands and carries it to the ambo, walking after the candlebearers, if candles are used.

If the deacon will read the Gospel from the lectionary already at the ambo, he stands before the celebrant at the proper time with hands joined, bows and asks the blessing; then he proceeds to the ambo. The deacon does not say the prayer: ALMIGHTY GOD, CLEANSE MY HEART. . . . Should he pass before the tabernacle he genuflects as he goes by.

Another priest, who performs the duties of the deacon, does not ask the blessing; but, bowing profoundly before the altar, says the prayer: ALMIGHTY GOD, CLEANSE MY HEART. . . . , and then goes to the ambo.

At the ambo the deacon, or other priest, with hands joined, greets the people, saying: THE LORD BE WITH YOU. After their response, he makes a small cross with his right thumb on the text and then on his forehead, lips and breast, saying aloud: A READING FROM THE HOLY GOSPEL . . . If incense is used, he now incenses the book, and then proclaims the Gospel. At its end he adds: THIS IS THE GOSPEL OF THE LORD, kisses the text and says: MAY THE WORDS OF THE GOSPEL. . . . He returns to his chair or, if no homily follows, he may remain at the ambo to announce the intentions of the general intercessions.

After the introduction to the general intercessions, the deacon announces the intentions and remains at the ambo while the celebrant says the concluding prayer.

# LITURGY OF THE EUCHARIST

After the general intercessions the deacon goes to the altar where, assisted by the acolytes, he spreads the corporal, places the chalice and the sacramentary on the altar. The chalice veil is left folded at the credence table. If there is a procession of gifts, the deacon assists the celebrant to accept the gifts from the faithful; otherwise he awaits the celebrant at the altar.

When the celebrant has come to the altar, the deacon hands him the paten with the hosts and uncovers the ciborium. Then he prepares the chalice, pouring into it the wine and a little water, and hands the chalice to the celebrant. As he pours the water into the chalice he says the prayer: BY THE MYSTERY OF. . . . The deacon may prepare the chalice either at the altar or at the credence table.

If incense is used, the deacon assists the celebrant as usual and may accompany him as he incenses the altar. Then the deacon incenses the celebrant and the people, in accord with local custom. After the incensing, the deacon assumes his position near the celebrant but a couple of steps back, where he remains, moving forward to minister at the book or at the chalice as needed. During the doxology the deacon elevates the chalice as the priest elevates the paten with the hosts. He makes the response: AMEN, with the people.

After the greeting, THE PEACE OF THE LORD . . . , the deacon says aloud the invitation to the sign of peace and exchanges the sign with the celebrant and with the ministers who are close by.

The deacon receives Holy Communion under both kinds from the celebrant. As usual, the celebrant says: THE BODY OF CHRIST or THE BLOOD OF CHRIST or THE BODY AND BLOOD OF CHRIST. The deacon responds: AMEN and receives the Sacrament. The deacon may assist the celebrant to distribute Communion to the faithful[86].

After Communion the deacon performs the ablutions in the usual manner, either at the altar or at the credence table. Or, the deacon may cover the vessels and leave them on a corporal at the credence table to be washed after Mass when the people have left[87].

---

[86] See pages 55-60.
[87] Cfr. Gen. Instr., n. 138.

The deacon then returns to the side of the celebrant. After the prayer after communion, the deacon may make brief remarks or announcements, if need be; when the celebrant has blessed the congregation, the deacon sings or says the dismissal.

The deacon goes with the celebrant to kiss the altar and, with him, makes the proper reverence to the altar. He walks at the side of the celebrant in the procession from the sanctuary.

# The Lector

The lector is instituted to proclaim the Scripture readings with the exception of the Gospel. He may also announce the intentions of the general intercessions and, in the absence of a cantor of the psalm, sing or read the psalm between the readings. The lector, although a layman, has his own proper function in the Eucharistic celebration and should exercise this even though ministers of higher rank are present. It is necessary that those who exercise the ministry of reading, even if they have not received institution, be qualified and carefully prepared so that the reading should develop in the faifthful a profound appreciation of the Scripture[88].

The lectionary should be prepared in advance with the markers carefully placed at the proper readings.

## INTRODUCTORY RITES

When the procession is about to leave the sacristy, the lector takes the lectionary with both hands and walks before the deacon or, if there is no deacon, before the celebrant. If he does not carry

---

[88] Cfr. Gen. Instr., n. 66 revised. For the manner of carrying the book in procession see page 4.

the lectionary, he should hold the hands joined. Reaching the sanctuary, the lector makes the proper reverence to the altar and goes to place the lectionary on the ambo, or he goes directly to his place. During the introductory rites the lector joins with the people in saying the responses and other parts assigned them.

# LITURGY OF THE WORD

After the opening prayer, the lector goes to the ambo. He reads the first reading and, at its end, adds: THIS IS THE WORD OF THE LORD. He may sit while the cantor sings the responsorial psalm or he may read it, in the absence of a cantor, remaining at the ambo. If a second reading is to be added, the lector comes to the ambo and reads it, as he did the first reading. If the cantor or the choir does not sing the Alleluia/verse of the Gospel, the lector sings them. Then he returns to his place.

If for any reason the deacon does not announce the intentions of the general intercessions, the lector proposes the intentions after the celebrant's introduction. Then he returns to his place. He may, in the course of the celebration, assist the other ministers as needed.

When the Mass is ended, the lector comes before the altar, makes the proper reverence and walks in the procession from the sanctuary.

It may be useful to add here that a non-catholic minister may not be invited to read one of the

Scripture readings and/or to preach during the celebration of Mass. This ruling is based on the provision of the Ecumenical Directory (n. 56), namely: A separated brother is not to act as a Scripture reader or to preach during the celebration of the Eucharist.

# The Acolyte

The acolyte[89] is instituted to serve at the altar and to assist the priest and deacon. In particular he prepares the altar and the vessels and, as auxiliary minister of the Eucharist, he gives Holy Communion to the faithful[90].

Laymen, even if they have not received institution as ministers, may perform all the functions below those reserved to deacons[91].

In view of the expanded role of the laity in the sacred liturgy, it is fitting to encourage some men of the parish to exercise the role of server at Holy Mass. These men could be enlisted from the pool of former altarboys and they would have no problem re-assuming their services at the altar. The service of these men would be most appropriate especially on Sundays and on Holy Days.

The present altarboys should be encouraged not to drop out after the eighth grade or after high school; rather they should be urged to continue their service to the priest and to God's people as dedicated and responsible young adults. The han-

---

[89] The functions of the installed acolyte are given in Study Text 3, The Ministries of the Church, pp. 35-36, published by the Bishops Committee on the Liturgy.

[90] Cfr. Gen. Instr., n. 65 revised.

[91] Cfr. Gen. Instr., n. 70.

dling of the sacred vessels and linens now called for at the beginning of the Liturgy of the Eucharist and after Communion surely suggest the need for older and more experienced ministers rather than small boys.

The acolyte wears the alb or a surplice over the cassock or, if a layman, he wears becoming lay attire. The 'monastic robe and cowl', popular these days, has little to recommend it outside of monastery churches. The acolyte is not a little monk.

Two acolytes should normally be assigned to each celebration; a larger number may be assigned, depending on their availability and the solemnity of the occasion. When the crucifix is carried, at least three acolytes are needed.

When moving about or standing still the acolytes should hold the hands joined, unless holding some object; it is most unsightly to see the ministers in the sanctuary with the hands dangling at their sides.

In the following lines the word 'acolyte' includes all the servers, whether men or boys, instituted or not.

# INTRODUCTORY RITES

A few minutes before the Mass begins, the acolytes light the candles at the altar and at the tabernacle, and see that everything is readied in the sanctuary. To light the candles the acolytes come before the altar, make the proper reverence — bow or genuflection —, and proceed to light the candles. They make a genuflection at the tabernacle. After lighting the candles they make the reverence to the altar again before returning to the sacristy.

The acolytes walk two by two before the clergy in the entrance procession. Entering the sanctuary they make the proper reverence and go to their places. The acolytes who carry the candles walk on either side of the crossbearer in the procession and, upon entering the sanctuary, go to put the candles in their place — either at the altar or on the credence table. Then they go to their chairs. If these same two acolytes have other functions in the Mass, they may remain standing by the credence table. In the absence of the deacon, the acolytes will have chairs on either side of the celebrant's chair. When the celebrant makes his reverence to the altar, these two acolytes make their reverence.

If necessary, one of the acolytes holds the sacramentary before the celebrant. During the introductory rites the acolytes join with the people in the responses and other parts assigned to them.

If the ceremony of blessing and sprinkling holy water is had, one of the acolytes brings the container of water to the celebrant after the greeting and holds it for the blessing. When the water has been blessed, an acolyte presents the aspergill to the deacon or to the celebrant. In the absence of the deacon, the acolyte may accompany the priest when he goes to bless the people. When the ceremony is ended, the acolyte puts aside the container of blessed water and the aspergill. Should the celebrant wish to mix salt in the water, the acolyte sees to it that the container of salt is presented to the priest at the proper time.

# LITURGY OF THE WORD

During the proclamation of the readings the acolytes sit at their places and listen attentively to God's Word.

At the Alleluia of the Gospel the two acolytes take their candles and stand near the thurifer; they follow him in the procession to the ambo. If the deacon, or other priest who reads the Gospel, genuflects at the tabernacle or bows at the altar as he passes, the acolytes merely pause. At the ambo they stand, facing each other, on either side of it. When the Gospel is ended, the acolytes put their candles on the credence table and return to their chairs, where, seated, they give their attention to the homily. They stand if the profession of faith is said, and for the general intercessions.

# LITURGY OF THE EUCHARIST

When the general intercessions have ended, the acolytes assist the deacon to prepare the altar, bringing to him various things needed. In the absence of the deacon, they themselves prepare the altar. They bring the stand with the sacramentary on it to the altar and place it a little to the left of center on the mensa; they place the corporal on the altar, unfolding it and spreading it at the center; they put the chalice with the purificator and the pall, if used, at the right end of the mensa. The veil of the chalice should be removed before taking the chalice to the altar and left, folded, on the credence table.

If it is customary, they assist the deacon or the

priest when he accepts the gifts from the faithful, putting them each in its assigned place. The cruets are placed on the credence table; the altarbreads and/or the ciborium are placed on the altar. The acolytes may carry the paten with the altarbreads and the ciborium, if these are on the credence table, to the celebrant when he comes to the altar and hand him first the ciborium and then the paten. Then they bring to the altar the cruets of wine and water and present them to the priest as he needs them. They should keep the handles of the cruets turned towards the priest. The acolyte may not pour water into the chalice at this time. If incense is used, the acolytes may assist the celebrant in the absence of the deacon as the priest blesses the incense and may accompany him as he goes around the altar.

After the incensing or, if it is not used, after the chalice is prepared, the acolytes bring the lavabo-bowl and towel, or the ewer of water and the basin and towel, for the washing of the priest's hands. Then they return to their chairs. The acolytes should not remain by the altar; during the Liturgy of the Eucharist only concelebrants may stand around the altar.

If it the custom, one of the acolytes may sound the handbell a little before the consecration and again at each raising of the consecrated Species.

# COMMUNION RITE

After the deacon has received Holy Communion, the acolytes who wish to receive, come to the altar two by two and with the hands joined; they may stand or kneel in accord with local custom.

Only the acolyte who has been duly instituted in the Ministry of Acolyte[92] may, as an extraordinary minister of the Eucharist, assist the celebrant to distribute the Sacrament to the faithful or to minister the chalice.

An acolyte with the Communion paten accompanies the minister when he distributes Communion to the faithful and, if both Species are administered, the acolytes accompany the appropriate minister and carry the paten, the silver tubes or spoons, etc., according to the method of Communion under both kinds being used[93]. After Communion these items, along with the paten, are left at the altar (the right end of the mensa) or at the credence table, depending on where the ablutions will take place. Then they return to their chairs.

At the prayer after Communion all stand. When the celebrant blesses the congregation, the acolytes, still standing, bless themselves, making a profound bow as they do so and adding the response: AMEN.

After the dismissal, the candlebearers take their candles in hand and accompany the crossbearer in the procession from the sanctuary. The other acolytes come from their places in twos, make the proper reverence to the altar and follow the candlebearers in the procession to the sacristy.

The acolytes extinguish the candles before removing the cassock and surplice.

---

[92] See appendix, n. 23.
[93] See Communion under Both Species, pp. 55 ff.

# The Thurifer

The thurifer is the acolyte whose responsibility it is to light the charcoals for the censer before Mass and to keep them burning, lest the symbolism of the incense be lost by the lack of fragrant clouds of smoke rising heavenward[94].

The thurifer carries the censer with his right hand and the incense-boat with the left, if necessary, and holds the chains near the top or by the attached rings. He should keep the lid of the censer slightly raised and swing the center gently to keep the coals alive.

The thurifer should consult with the priest before Mass to determine when he wishes to use the incense. It may be used at any or at all those parts of the Mass indicated in the General Instruction[95]: at the entrance procession, at the veneration of the altar, at the Gospel, at the preparation of the gifts and at the Consecrations.

A. PROCESSION AND VENERATION OF THE ALTAR. In the sacristy, when the ministers

---

[94] Incense at Mass is rated, along with the lights, vestments, etc., by the Council of Trent, as one of "those visible signs of religion and piety" which elevate the minds of the faithful to devout contemplation. (Sess. 22, Ch. V.)

[95] Cfr. Gen. Instr., n. 235 revised; also Use of Incense, appendix, n. 3.

have vested, the thurifer brings the censer (and boat) to the celebrant, opens it sufficiently and holds it for him to put in and bless the incense. Then he closes the censer and takes his place in front of the acolytes with candles for the procession to the sanctuary. On entering the sanctuary, the thurifer goes to stand near the altar where he can conveniently present the censer to the deacon or to the priest. When the priest has kissed the altar, the thurifer goes to him and hands him (or the deacon) the censer. In the absence of the deacon, the thurifer may accompany the priest to incense the altar. He then takes the censer to the sacristy and returns to his assigned chair in the sanctuary.

B. THE GOSPEL. Before the *Alleluia* the thurifer goes to the sacristy. He sees if the charcoals are alive; if not, he re-lights them. When the *Alleluia* begins, the thurifer takes the censer to the celebrant and, as before, holds it open for the blessing. The thurifer then stands back to allow the deacon to ask the blessing, then turns and leads the candlebearers and the deacon to the ambo. Should the deacon bow to the altar as he passes it, the thurifer does likewise. If another priest or the celebrant himself reads the Gospel, the thurifer stops behind him as he bows to say the prayer before the altar.

At the ambo, the thurifer stands on the right side and, at the proper time, presents the censer to the minister. After the incensing, the thurifer takes the censer to the sacristy and returns to his chair to listen to the homily.

C. PREPARATION OF THE GIFTS. After the general intercessions, the thurifer goes to the sacristy and makes sure the charcoals are alive. At the proper time he takes the censer to the celebrant and holds it, as before, for the blessing. In the absence of the deacon, he may accompany the priest when he incenses the altar; then he may incense the priest and the people. When the deacon incenses the priest and the people, the thurifer stands at his side. He then takes the censer to the sacristy.

D. THE CONSECRATIONS. The thurifer puts incense on the charcoals before bringing the censer to the sanctuary a few moments before the Consecration. He kneels in front of the altar and incenses the Host and the chalice with the Precious Blood as each is shown to the people. Then he rises, genuflects and takes the censer to the sacristy. When incensing the sacred Species, he swings the censer with three double-swings. The thurifer should return to the sanctuary and remain at his place for the remainder of the Mass. He receives Holy Communion with the other acolytes.

After the dismissal, the thurifer makes the proper reverence to the altar and walks, with hands joined, in front of the candlebearers in the procession to the sacristy.

# Concelebration[96]

Concelebration of the Eucharist aptly demonstrates the unity of the sacrifice and of the priesthood[97].

The occasions when concelebration is required or permitted are set forth in nn. 76, 153-154 and 157-158 of the General Instruction on the Roman Missal, and in the Declaration on Concelebration issued by the Sacred Congregation for Divine Worship on August 7, 1972[98].

On Christmas Day the priest may concelebrate three Masses, provided they are celebrated at the proper times: at midnight, at dawn and during the day[99]. They may not be concelebrated one immediately after the other.

When the Bishop is present, he should preside over the assembly by associating the priests with himself in concelebration, or by conducting the Liturgy of the Word and the Rite of Dismissal.

No additional concelebrants may be admitted to

---

[96] See 'Concelebration', an explanation by the Bishops Committee on Liturgy, Newsletter, June 1966.
[97] IEW, n. 47. See also CSL, nn. 41 and 57; and Conciliar Decree on Priestly Life and Ministry, n. 7, par. 1, and n. 8, par. 4.
[98] Newsletter, Feb. 1973, p. 3; Notitiae, Nov. 1972, p. 327.
[99] Cfr. Gen. Instr., n. 158,c.

concelebrate once the Mass has begun[100].

Normally each priest-concelebrant wears all the vestments prescribed for a priest celebrating individually. The principal celebrant always wears vestments of the color proper to the liturgical celebration; the concelebrants, if necessary, wear white vestments, except in the unlikely case of Mass for the Dead when the principal celebrant wears black or violet vestments. If a sufficient number of suitable chasubles is not at hand, the concelebrants may wear the alb and the stole, omitting the chasuble. The principal celebrant always wears the chasuble[101].

"The practice of wearing only a stole over the monastic cowl (or religious habit) or ordinary clerical garb for concelebration is reproved as an abuse"[102].

In general the principal celebrant observes the same ceremonies (gestures and prayers) as he would when celebrating alone, noting the few exceptions indicated in the rite. The concelebrants observe only those ceremonies (gestures and prayers) that are assigned to them in the Liturgy of the Eucharist.

When prayers are sung or said in unison by the principal celebrant and the concelebrants, the voice of the former should be clearly heard by the faithful over the voices of the latter[103].

---

[100] Cfr. Gen. Instr., n. 156.
[101] Cfr. Gen. Instr., n. 16.
[102] See appendix, n. 1.
[103] Cfr. Gen. Instr., n. 170, and Newsletter, Feb. 1973, p. 4, Commentary.

The deacon and the lector, when available, should exercise their proper functions. In their absence, several of the concelebrants perform the duties of the deacon and of the lector.

# PREPARATIONS

The altar is readied as for any Mass with a white cloth and at least two candles. The crucifix should be near the altar, or carried in the entrance procession and placed before the altar. The sacramentary and, if needed, a book of chants, should be placed near the principal celebrant's chair; the lectionary is readied at the ambo, unless it is carried in the entrance procession.

The following items are readied on the credence table:

a) the chalice or chalices, with corporals, purificators and, if used, the pall; b) the bowl and ewer of water and the towel for the Lavabo, and the vessel of water for purifying the fingers after Communion; c) the stand for the sacramentary.

If there will be no procession of gifts, the following should be readied on the credence table: the larger host[104] or several large hosts for the celebrants on a paten, and the ciborium of smaller hosts for the faithful, the cruets of wine and water; also, if they will be needed, silver tubes or the spoon for Communion at the chalice, and the vessel of water for cleansing them, as noted in Communion under both Species, pp. 55-60. If, on a Sunday, there will be the ceremony of blessing and sprinkling

---

[104] Cfr. IEW, n. 48.

holy water, these additional items will be readied: the vessel of water to be blessed and the vessel of salt, if used, and the aspergill.

If it would be more convenient, the chalices may be readied with the wine already in them on the credence table, leaving the water to be added at the altar or, when this is done by the deacon or by one of the concelebrants, at the credence table.

Chairs for the concelebrants should be prepared in the sanctuary, if space permits; otherwise they occupy the front pews. Copies of the text of the Eucharistic Prayer to be used should be readied for the concelebrants.

In the sacristy or elsewhere, if necessary:

a) vestments for the principal celebrant: alb, stole, chasuble;

b) vestments for the concelebrants: albs, stoles (chasubles);

c) vestments for the deacon: alb, stole (dalmatic);

d) albs or surplices for the other ministers[105].

If incense is used, the same procedures are observed as described for any Mass[106].

# INTRODUCTORY RITES

When the ministers are vested, each according to his order or function, the principal celebrant may bless the incense, and the procession moves through the church to the sanctuary.

When they reach the sanctuary, the servers with the censer, the cross and the candles proceed as

---
[105] See appendix, n. 1.
[106] See appendix, n. 3.

described on page 5; other participating ministers and clergy make the proper reverence and go to their places; the deacon, concelebrants and the principal celebrant make the proper reverence, kiss the altar and go to their places. All remain standing.

If incense is used, the principal celebrant, after kissing the altar, receives the censer from the deacon or other minister and incenses the altar and crucifix as usual.

The principal celebrant presides during the introductory rites in the same manner as described on pages 8-15. If there was no entrance hymn and others did not sing or read the antiphon, the Introit antiphon given in the Mass formulary is recited by the concelebrants; the principal celebrant remains silent. The concelebrants join with the people in singing or saying the penitential rite, the Kyrie, the Gloria, the profession of faith and in all the responses.

If, at a funeral Mass, the casket is received by the priest at the door of the church just prior to the Mass, the greeting is not repeated at the chair and the penitential rite/Kyrie are omitted. After the priest kisses the altar at the beginning, he goes to the chair and sings/says the opening prayer[107].

After the opening prayer and the response, all sit and listen attentively to the readings, participate in the responsorial psalm and sing the Alleluia and verse. All stand when the Alleluia begins and remain standing during the Gospel, the profession of faith, if said, and the general intercessions.

---

[107] Newsletter, Apr.-May 1971, p. 3.

# LITURGY OF THE WORD

The Liturgy of the Word is celebrated in the same manner as described on pages 15-25. However:

a) in the absence of the lector and the deacon, one of the concelebrants proclaims the readings before the Gospel, the responsorial psalm and the *Alleluia*/verse. This last should be omitted if it is not sung.

b) in the absence of the deacon, one of the concelebrants proclaims the Gospel; he does not ask the blessing (even if the Ordinary presides), but he stands before the altar, makes a profound bow and says the prayer: ALMIGHTY GOD, CLEANSE MY HEART. . . . Then he proceeds to read the Gospel as usual. The principal celebrant should not proclaim the Gospel.[108]

c) one of the concelebrants may give the homily.

d) in the absence of the lector and the deacon, one of the concelebrants reads the intentions of the general intercessions.

# LITURGY OF THE EUCHARIST

After the general intercessions all sit while the deacon or two of the concelebrants prepare the altar as usual.

If there is a procession of gifts, the deacon or a concelebrant assists the principal celebrant to accept the gifts from the faithful. At the altar the principal celebrant, assisted by the deacon or by concelebrants, proceeds with the preparation of the

---

[108] Cfr. Gen. Instr., n. 160.

gifts as described on pages 27-31. For concelebration the use of larger altarbreads, which can easily be broken for the Communion of the concelebrants, is commendable[109]. Otherwise, several large altarbreads should be used.

After washing and drying his hands the principal celebrant, slowly extending and rejoining the hands, says the invitation to pray: PRAY, BRETHREN, . . . All make the response.

Just before the prayer over the gifts[110], the concelebrants take their place around the altar, if space permits without crowding, being careful not to stand between the altar and the congregation. Then the principal celebrant extends his hands and sings or says the prayer over the gifts. All respond: AMEN. The concelebrants should have in hand the text of the Eucharistic prayer.

Practical difficulties may arise when the number of concelebrants is exceptionally high and several possible solutions are suggested in Newsletter, Feb. 1973 (page 4, Commentary):

1) If the area around the altar is adequate to accomodate the entire group conveniently, all may

---

[109] IEW, n. 48.

[110] There seems to be two schools of thought as to when the concelebrants come to the altar. The one proposed here is taken from the *Ritus Servandus in Concelebratione Missae* (nn. 36 and 39) and from the ceremonial of Father Braga, one of the architects of the revised liturgy: *LA CELEBRAZIONE EUCARISTICA*. Another opinion which suggests the concelebrants come to the altar after the prayer over the gifts is proposed by Father J. Patino, in THE NEW ORDER OF MASS.

exercise their ministry at the altar, taking care not to interfere with the ministry of the deacon who assists the celebrant.

2) If the area around the altar is not adequate to accommodate the group conveniently, a representative part of the group may exercise their ministry within the sanctuary area, and the other concelebrants should occupy the first rows in the church — where they remain for the entire celebration.

This latter suggestion accords perfectly with the statement in the Declaration on Concelebration issued by the Sacred Congregation for Divine Worship, namely: "It is fitting that priests, by reason of their ordination, celebrate or concelebrate Mass so that they may participate more fully and in the manner proper to them, and not only communicate like the laity[111].

However, if they do not concelebrate ritually, the priests present may communicate under both Species.

# EUCHARISTIC PRAYER

The principal celebrant and the concelebrants do not recite together the entire Eucharistic prayer[112].

The preface is sung or said by the principal celebrant alone; the concelebrants join in the responses and in the Sanctus. The concelebrants stand

---

[111] Declaration on Concelebration, opening paragraphs. See Appendix, n. 30.

[112] See 'Simultaneous Recitation', Newsletter, June 1972, p. 1. See Appendix n. 12.

throughout the entire Eucharistic prayer.

The gestures which accompany the Consecration and the doxology are common to all four Eucharistic prayers, hence they are described but once.

# THE WORD OF INSTITUTION OR THE CONSECRATIONS

The gestures of the principal celebrant at this part of the Mass are the same as those described on page 36. He should speak in a voice loud enough to be heard by the people over the voices of the others and to lead the concelebrants in reciting the words with him.

As they and the principal celebrant repeat the very words of Christ, the concelebrants may extend the right hand towards the altar; they look at the Body of Christ when it is raised; they make a profound bow when the principal celebrant genuflects.

When they, with the principal celebrant, say the words: WHEN SUPPER WAS ENDED. . . . . . , the concelebrants keep the hands joined; when they repeat the very words of Christ, they may extend the right hand towards the altar; they look at the chalice with the Precious Blood when it is raised; they make a profound bow when the principal celebrant genuflects.

The extension of the right hand at the words of institution is optional; it should be agreed beforehand whether or not to perform this gesture. The words of institution may be sung.

The principal celebrant, alone, voices the invitation to proclaim the Mystery of Faith; the concelebrants join with the people in the acclamation. If none of the faithful is present to make the acclamation, it is omitted[113]. The invitation and the acclamation may be sung.

# DOXOLOGY

The doxology concludes the Eucharistic prayer; it may be sung or said by the principal celebrant alone, or by all the celebrants with the principal celebrant. No one else in the assembly — whether deacon, other minister or laity — may join in singing or saying the doxology. The people respond: AMEN. During the entire doxology, including the people's response, the paten with the Host on it is raised by the principal celebrant and the chalice is raised by the deacon or, in his absence, by one of the concelebrants.

In the course of each Eucharistic prayer the names of the Pope and of the Ordinary of the place are mentioned[114]. In the following paragraphs the phrase, 'all the celebrants', includes the principal celebrant and the concelebrants.

# EUCHARISTIC PRAYER I
*(Roman Canon)*

WE COME TO YOU, FATHER..... (*Te igitur*) is said by the principal celebrant alone, and he alone makes the sign of the cross indicated in the prayer.

---

[113] Newsletter, Oct.-Nov. 1969, p. 7.
[114] See page 38.

The Intercessions for the Church and the Commemoration of the Living may be said either by the principal celebrant alone or by one of the concelebrants with his hands extended. If a special Communicantes is prescribed, it must be used.

FATHER, ACCEPT THIS OFFERING . . . is said by the principal celebrant alone. When a special Hanc Igitur is prescribed, he must use it.

The following prayers are recited by all the celebrants together.

BLESS AND APPROVE OUR OFFERINGS. . . . . . , and the concelebrants extend both hands (palms down) toward the altar. This gesture of extending the hands is obligatory[115]. This prayer may be sung.

THE DAY BEFORE HE SUFFERED. . . . . . ; and during it the concelebrants may extend the right hand toward the altar when they repeat the words of institution. This prayer may be sung.

The consecration of the bread and of the wine follow, as described above.

FATHER, WE CELEBRATE THE MEMORY. . . . . is recited by all the celebrants with the hands extended. This prayer may be sung.

LOOK WITH FAVOR. . . . . . is said by all the celebrants, and the prayer may be sung.

ALMIGHTY GOD, WE PRAY THAT YOUR ANGEL. . . . . is said by all the celebrants with the hands joined and head bowed; they stand erect and bless themselves at the words: LET US BE FILLED. . . . . This prayer may be sung.

---

[115] Cfr. Gen. Instr., n. 174, a): *"Manibus ad oblata extensis"*.

Here the recitation by all the celebrants together ends.

REMEMBER, LORD, THOSE WHO HAVE DIED. . . . . and FOR OURSELVES, TOO, WE ASK. . . . . may be said either by the principal celebrant alone or by one of the concelebrants with his hands extended. At the words: THOUGH WE ARE SINNERS, all strike the breast once.

THROUGH CHRIST OUR LORD YOU GIVE US. . . . . is said by the principal celebrant alone. The doxology follows, as described above.

# EUCHARISTIC PRAYER II

The principal celebrant alone sings or says the preface.

LORD, YOU ARE HOLY INDEED, THE FOUNTAIN OF ALL HOLINESS, is said by the principal celebrant alone.

The following prayers are recited by all the celebrants together.

LET YOUR SPIRIT COME UPON. . . . . . is said by all the celebrants. The concelebrants extend both hands towards the altar while saying this prayer. They keep them so extended when the principal celebrant makes the sign of the cross over the gifts, but join them when they say: BEFORE HE WAS GIVEN UP TO DEATH, A DEATH HE FREELY ACCEPTED. All these prayers may be sung.

The consecration of the bread and of the wine follows, as described above.

IN MEMORY OF HIS DEATH. . . . . is said by all the celebrants with the hands extended.

This prayer may be sung.

Here the recitation by all the celebrants together ends.

LORD, REMEMBER YOUR CHURCH. . . . . and REMEMBER OUR BROTHERS. . . . . may be said either by the principal celebrant or by one of the concelebrants with his hands extended. The hands are joined at: . . . THROUGH YOUR SON, JESUS CHRIST. The doxology follows, as described above.

# EUCHARISTIC PRAYER III

FATHER, YOU ARE HOLY INDEED. . . . . . is said by the principal celebrant alone.

The following prayers are recited by all the celebrants together.

AND SO, FATHER, WE BRING YOU THESE GIFTS. . . . . . . is said by all the celebrants; the concelebrants extend both hands (palms down) toward the altar and keep them extended through the words: . . . WE CELEBRATE THIS EUCHARIST.

ON THE NIGHT HE WAS BETRAYED. . . . . is said by all the celebrants. It may be sung.

The consecration of the bread and the wine follows, as described above.

FATHER, CALLING TO MIND THE DEATH . . . . . to . . . . AND BECOME ONE BODY, ONE SPIRIT IN CHRIST, is said by all the celebrants, with the hands extended. This prayer may be sung.

Here the recitation by all the celebrants together ends.

MAY HE MAKE US AN EVERLASTING

GIFT TO YOU. . . . . and LORD, MAY THIS SACRIFICE. . . . . are said either by the principal celebrant alone or by one of the concelebrants with his hands extended. The hands are joined at the words: WE HOPE TO ENJOY . . . . . . GOOD THINGS TO COME.

The doxology follows, as described above.

# EUCHARISTIC PRAYER IV

This Eucharistic prayer has an inseparable preface; it may not be used with any other preface, nor may it be used in any celebration that calls for a proper preface. The preface is sung or said by the principal celebrant alone; the concelebrants join with the people in the responses and in the Sanctus.

FATHER, WE ACKNOWLEDGE YOUR GREATNESS. . . . . . is said by the principal celebrant alone.

FATHER, MAY THIS HOLY SPIRIT. . . . . is recited by all the celebrants; the concelebrants extend both hands (palms down) toward the altar and keep them extended through the words: BECOME THE BODY AND BLOOD OF JESUS CHRIST OUR LORD. With the hands joined they continue: AS WE CELEBRATE. . . . . .

HE ALWAYS LOVED THOSE WHO. . . . . . is said by all the celebrants; as they say the words: TAKE THIS, ALL OF YOU. . . , the concelebrants may extend the right hand towards the altar. All of the prayers, from FATHER, WE ACKNOWLEDGE. . . . . and the words of institution, may be sung.

The consecration of the bread and of the wine follows, as described above.

FATHER, WE NOW CELEBRATE THE MEMORIAL. . . . . . is said by all the celebrants with the hands extended. This prayer may be sung.

LORD, LOOK UPON THIS SACRIFICE. . . . . . is said by all the celebrants.

Here the recitation by all the celebrants together ends.

LORD, REMEMBER THOSE FOR WHOM. . . . . . . is said either by the principal celebrant or by one of the concelebrants with the hands extended; the hands are joined at the conclusion: THROUGH WHOM YOU GIVE US EVERYTHING THAT IS GOOD. The doxology follows, as described above.

For those who concelebrate in Latin the booklet, PRECES EUCHARISTICAE PRO CONCELEBRATIONE, will prove helpful. It contains the texts and the rubrics as well as the chant for the parts that may be sung. An English version is available: EUCHARISTIC PRAYERS FOR CONCELEBRATION. It contains no chant.

# COMMUNION RITE

The principal celebrant alone, with the hands joined, sings or says the introduction to the Lord's Prayer. He alone extends the hands while all the celebrants and the people pray the OUR FATHER. He alone says the embolism; and joins his hands while the concelebrants and the people make the acclamation.

The principal celebrant alone says the prayer for

peace. Then slowly extending and rejoining his hands, the principal celebrant alone gives the peace-greeting to the assembly. If the exchange of the sign of peace takes place, the deacon or, in his absence, one of the concelebrants sings or says: LET US OFFER. . . . . ; the principal celebrant exchanges the sign of peace with the concelebrants nearest to himself and then with the deacon, without leaving his position at the altar.

During the singing of the AGNUS DEI, the principal celebrant, assisted, if need be, by the concelebrants, breaks the Hosts for the Communion of the celebrants. The principal celebrant drops a small portion into the chalice, saying: MAY THIS MINGLING. . . . . , and says the prayer of preparation for his Communion.

The Lord's Body is distributed to the concelebrants in one of the following ways:

a) the principal celebrant genuflects, steps back a little. Each concelebrant comes to the altar, genuflects, takes a particle with the right hand and, holding the left hand under the right, returns to his place;

b) the concelebrants remain at their places. The paten with the particles on it is passed from one to the other and each takes a particle. No genuflection is made;

c) the concelebrants remain at their places. The principal celebrant or one of the concelebrants moves among them carrying the paten from which each takes a particle. No genuflection is made.

When all the concelebrants have the particle, the principal celebrant takes the Host with the right hand and holds the paten under It with the left.

He raises both, saying: THIS IS THE LAMB OF GOD. . . . and HAPPY ARE THOSE WHO. . . . . Then all the celebrants join with the people to say the act of humility: LORD, I AM NOT WORTHY. . . . . Then the principal celebrant says; MAY THE BODY OF CHRIST. . . . . , and he and the concelebrants reverently consume the Body of Christ. The principal celebrant then gives Communion with the Host to the deacon in the usual manner.

The principal celebrant then communicates at the chalice in the usual manner, unless silver tubes or the spoon is used, as noted below. The concelebrants may receive the Lord's Blood in one of the following ways:

## 1). directly from the chalice:

a) after the principal celebrant has received, he wipes the outside of the chalice with the purificator and hands the chalice to the deacon or to one of the concelebrants. He then goes to give Communion to the faithful or returns to the chair. The concelebrants come to the altar one by one or in pairs if two chalices are used. They drink the Lord's Blood and return to their seats. The deacon or the concelebrant wipes the chalice with a purificator after each one communicates.

b) The concelebrants remain at their places. The deacon or the concelebrant, or even the principal celebrant, offers the chalice to each one or it may be passed from one to the other. The chalice is always wiped with a purificator either by the one who is offering it or by the one who drinks from it. After communicating the concelebrants return to their seats.

## 2). With silver tubes.

The principal celebrant also uses the silver tube, purifying it after he has received the Lord's Blood with some water from the container on the altar. He then places the tube on a paten. The deacon or one of the concelebrants places the chalice in the middle of the altar or at the right side on another corporal. A container of water for washing the tubes is placed near the chalice, with a paten to hold them afterwards. The concelebrants come forward one by one, take a tube and drink a little. They then clean the tube with water and place it on the paten.

## 3). With the Spoon.

The principal celebrant also uses the spoon. The concelebrants receive the Lord's Blood in the same way as with the silver tubes.

The deacon receives Communion last, drinking what remains in the chalice and then taking it to the credence table where he washes and dries it, and covers it in the usual way. The acolyte carries the tubes or the spoon to the credence table where he washes and dries them.

Concelebrants may also receive from the chalice at the altar immediately after they receive the Lord's Body. In this case, the principal celebrant communicates under both kinds as usual, but he follows the same rite as the concelebrants for Communion from the chalice.

After the principal celebrant's Communion, the chalice is placed on another corporal at the right side of the altar. The concelebrants come forward one by one, genuflect, and receive the Lord's Body. Then they go to the side of the altar and drink the Lord's Blood following the same rite as the principal celebrant. The deacon receives last, drinking what remains in the chalice and washing it, as above.

The Communion may be received by intinction. In this case, the principal celebrant receives the Body and Blood of Christ in the usual way, making sure that enough remains in the chalice for the concelebrants. The deacon or one of the concelebrants arranges the paten with the particles and the chalice at the center of the altar or at the right side on another corporal. Each concelebrant comes to the altar, genuflects, and takes a particle; he dips the particle into the chalice and, holding a paten under his chin, reverently communicates. He then returns to his chair.

After the concelebrants, the deacon receives Communion in the same way, but from one of the concelebrants, who first says: THE BODY AND BLOOD OF CHRIST, to which the deacon replies: AMEN. At the altar then the deacon drinks all that remains in the chalice, takes it to the credence table, where he washes and dries it and covers it as usual.

The vessels may be left at the credence table — on a corporal — to be purified after Mass. They should be covered with the veil.

One or more of the concelebrants may assist in the distribution of the Sacrament to the faithful.

If they receive Communion under both Species, the deacon, or a concelebrant or an acolyte[116] ministers the chalice in the manner described on pages 55-60.

After Communion, all sit at their places for the period of silent reflection/thanksgiving as usual.

The principal celebrant, standing either at the chair or at the altar, invites the assembly to pray, saying: LET US PRAY. He may pause for a few moments if a period of silence did not precede; then, with his hands extended, sings or says the prayer after Communion. He joins his hands for the short conclusion. The assembly sings or says the response: AMEN.

If any other liturgical service follows immediately, the Mass ends at this point, with the blessing and the dismissal omitted.

The principal celebrant concludes the Mass in the usual way. He kisses the altar, if convenient[117]. The ministers, clergy and the principal celebrant make the usual reverence to the altar and walk in procession from the sanctuary.

---

[116] See footnote #75; Cfr. Gen. Instr., n. 238 revised.
[117] Cfr. Gen. Instr., n. 125 revised.

# Mass Without A Congregation
## MASS IN PRIVATE

Priests are urged to celebrate Mass every day, for even if the faithful are not present, it is an act of Christ and His Church[118].

A 'Mass in Private' is one celebrated by the priest with only the server to function and respond. It is not excluded, however, that others be present who do not participate.

Except for a good reason Mass should not be celebrated when a server is not available; but when the server is not available, the greetings throughout the Mass and the final blessing/dismissal are omitted[119].

When he celebrates Mass in private, the priest may use either the Latin or the English texts.

Each priest always retains his right to celebrate individually[120], but he may not celebrate Mass without a congregation on Holy Thursday and the Sacraments are not celebrated on Good Friday or on

---
[118] See Decree on Priestly Life and Ministry, n. 13; and IEW, n. 44.
[119] Cfr. Gen. Instr., n. 211.
[120] CSL, n. 57, 2,2.

The altar prepared for Mass. The lectern with the book at the left side of the altar and the veiled chalice at the right side of the altar.

Holy Saturday[121].

# PREPARATIONS

The altar is prepared as usual: a white cloth and two candles. Unless a larger crucifix dominates the altar, a small crucifix should be on the altar. The sacramentary is placed on the left side of the altar; the chalice, with purificator, pall, if used, and corporal, is covered with the veil and placed on the right side of the altar. The corporal is not unfolded until the preparation of the gifts. The chalice may be readied on a stand beside the altar.

Cruets of wine and water, the bowl and towel for the Lavabo, are placed on the credence table or on another stand by the altar, but not on the mensa.

The lectionary is readied near the left side of the altar. As at all Masses, the lectionary approved by the National Conference of Bishops and confirmed by the Holy See must be used.

The priest wears the same vestments that are prescribed for all Masses, as described on page 3[122].

# INTRODUCTORY RITES

The priest, after vesting in the proper vestments, goes to the altar, preceded by the server. Both make the same reverence — a profound bow or a genuflection, if the tabernacle is nearby. Both remain standing at the foot of the altar until after the penitential act.

---

[121] Cfr. Sacramentary, Easter Triduum.
[122] See Vesture, appendix, n. 1.

The Sign of the Cross, the greeting, the Confiteor take place at the foot of the altar.

The priest and the server make the sign of the cross. The priest says: IN THE NAME OF THE FATHER, . . . . . ; the server responds: AMEN.

The priest greets the server using one of the given formulas and the server makes the appropriate response. If there is no server, the greeting is omitted.

The invitation to the penitential act is omitted; the priest and the server, together, say at once the simplfied Confiteor, striking the breast (once) at the words: THROUGH MY OWN FAULT. . . . . The priest alone says the petition: MAY ALMIGHTY GOD HAVE MERCY. . . . . The server responds: AMEN. The revised Missale Romanum indicates that Form A, i.e., the Confiteor, be used at a Mass in private.

After the penitential act, the priest ascends to the altar, kisses it and moves to the left in front of the sacramentary. This is his place until the preparation of the gifts.

At the book the priest, with hands joined, reads the Introit antiphon, the *Kyrie,* alternating the invocations with the server, says together with the server the *GLORIA*, if prescribed, and/or says, with hands joined: LET US PRAY. After a momentary pause, he extends the hands and reads the opening prayer. He joins the hands for the (long) conclusion. The server responds: AMEN.

# LITURGY OF THE WORD

The Scripture readings before the Gospel are read by the server or by the priest; the priest remains at the altar in any case. The server may read

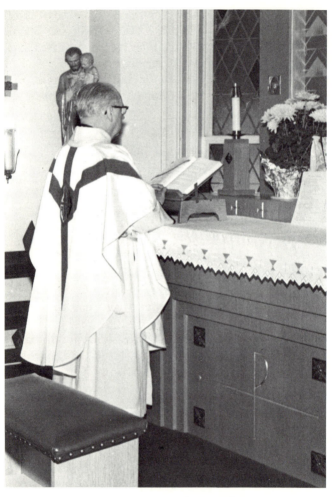

Standing at the left side of the altar the priest reads the Introit Antiphon, Kyrie, Gloria, the Oration, the Creed and the Universal Prayer. He remains here for the readings.

the readings at any suitable place. He also reads the responsorial psalm and the *Alleluia*/verse of the Gospel. The responsorial psalm may be read through, with the given response said only at the beginning and again at the end. The two readings before the Gospel are read on Sundays and on Holy Days.

The priest himself reads the Gospel. Standing at the book, the priest makes a profound bow and says the prayer: ALMIGHTY GOD, CLEANSE MY HEART . . . , and then reads the Gospel in the usual way. After the Gospel, the priest says: MAY THE WORDS OF THE GOSPEL. . . . . , and the server says the acclamation: PRAISE TO YOU, LORD JESUS CHRIST. The priest kisses the text of the Gospel.

The profession of faith, if prescribed, is said by the priest and the server, and both make a profound bow at the words: BY THE POWER OF THE HOLY SPIRIT HE WAS BORN OF THE VIRGIN MARY, AND BECAME MAN. On the feasts of the Annunciation and of Christmas, both make a genuflection at these words. The general intercessions may be added, since these are considered a normal part of the Mass[123]. When there is no server, the priest omits the introduction to the general intercessions and simply pauses momentarily after each intention. The formulas for general intercessions, found in the Appendix of the sacramentary, may conveniently be used.

---

[123] Cfr. Gen. Instr., n. 220.

# LITURGY OF THE EUCHARIST

When the Liturgy of the Word is ended, the priest moves to the center of the altar, the place of sacrifice. The server brings the chalice, if need be, but leaves the veil at the credence table or stand. The priest unfolds the corporal and spreads it at the center, takes the paten with the large altarbread on it[124], says the prayer of blessing and places the paten on the corporal. The server may make the response: BLESSED BE GOD FOREVER.

The priest goes to the right side of the altar to prepare the chalice, pouring into it the wine and a little water. He says the prayer: BY THE MYSTERY OF THIS WATER. . . . . Then he returns to the center where he holds the chalice as usual, saying the prayer of blessing. The server may respond.

The prayers and the gestures that accompany the preparation of the gifts and the Lavabo are the same as described on pages 29-30.

After the prayer: LORD GOD, WE ASK YOU TO. . . . . , the priest goes to the right side of the altar to wash his hands as usual. The server ministers the water and the towel. When he has no server, the priest may find it more convenient to use a bowl of water at the Lavabo.

At the center, the priest faces the server and

---

[124] A small altarbread may be placed on the paten for the server's Communion, or, and better, the priest may give a portion of the large altarbread to the server. (Cfr. Gen. Instr., n. 283.).

The priest stands at the right end of the altar for the Lavabo.

says the invitation: PRAY, BROTHER, THAT. . . . . . .[125], extending and rejoining his hands as he does so. The server makes the response. If there is no server, the invitation and the response are omitted.

The priest, with hands extended, says the prayer over the gifts. He joins his hands for the (short) conclusion. The server responds: AMEN.

The proclamation of the Eucharistic prayer follows in the same manner as at any Mass, as described on pages 31-45. The server makes all the responses and acclamations, and he recites the Sanctus with the priest. If there is no server, the acclamation after the Consecrations, along with its invitation, is omitted[126].

# COMMUNION RITE

After the doxology and the server's response, the priest, with hands joined, says the introduction to the Lord's Prayer. Then the priest and the server recite the OUR FATHER. . . . . . The priest adds the embolism with the hands still extended, but he joins them when the server says the acclamation: FOR THE KINGDOM. . . . . When there is no server, the priest omits this acclamation.

The priest says the prayer for peace as usual, then he faces the server and, extending and rejoining the hands, gives the peace-greeting: THE PEACE OF THE LORD. . . . . , to which the server

---

[125] When Mass is said in Latin, this invitation retains the plural form: *ORATE, FRATRES,* . . . . .

[126] Cfr. Gen. Instr., n. 211; also Newsletter, Oct.-Nov. 1969, p. 7, or *NOTITIAE*, 1969, p. 324.

The priest faces the minister at: Pray, brother; at the peace-greeting; at This is the Lamb of God. . . . ; and at the concluding rites.

responds: AND ALSO WITH YOU. The priest may exchange the sign of peace with the server.

The triple LAMB OF GOD. . . . is said by the priest and the server, and while saying it the priest breaks the Host as usual and drops a small portion of It into the chalice, saying: MAY THIS MINGLING. . . . . . The priest then makes his own preparation for Communion, saying one of the given prayers, and then he genuflects.

Whether or not the server will receive Holy Communion determines the action and the prayer that follow.

If the server will receive Holy Communion, the priest takes the Host with his right hand and the paten with the other and, facing the server, says: THIS IS THE LAMB OF GOD WHO TAKES. . . . . . and BLESSED ARE THOSE WHO. . . . . ; then together with the server the priest says: LORD, I AM NOT WORTHY. . . . . .

If the server will not receive Holy Communion, the priest, after genuflecting, takes the Host in hand and, facing the altar, says only the act of humility: LORD, I AM NOT WORTHY. . . . .

The priest reverently consumes the Body of the Lord as usual. The paten is not cleansed before consuming the Precious Blood, as before; this is done at the ablutions. Pausing only long enough to swallow the Host, the priest drinks from the chalice.

After he has consumed the Precious Blood, the priest reads the Communion antiphon in the text of the Mass and then gives the Sacrament to the server in the usual manner.

At the right side of the altar the priest does the ablutions. First he cleanses the paten over the chalice, if need be, and wipes it with the purificator; then he washes the chalice with wine and water or with water only, dries it and covers it as usual. The chalice, covered with the veil, may be left at the right side of the altar or taken by the server to the side table.

A period of silent reflection/thanksgiving may be observed with the priest standing at the center of the altar. Then, with hands joined, he says: LET US PRAY. He extends the hands as he reads the prayer after Communion, but joins them for the (short) conclusion. The server responds: AMEN.

# CONCLUSION

Facing the server, the priest slowly extends and rejoins his hands, saying: THE LORD BE WITH YOU. The server responds: AND ALSO WITH YOU. The priest blesses the server, making the sign of the cross and saying: MAY ALMIGHTY GOD BLESS YOU, THE FATHER, . . . . . Again the server says: AMEN. If there is no server, the greeting and the blessing are omitted.

The final greeting: GO IN PEACE. . . . is always omitted in a Mass without a congregation[127].

The priest kisses the altar, makes the proper reverence with the server and returns to the sacristy.

---

[127] Cfr. Gen. Instr., n. 231.

When there is no server, the Mass ends after the prayer after Communion. After concluding the prayer after Communion, the priest kisses the altar, and makes the proper reverence[128].

The priest who travels abroad and is not familiar with the local language, will find the *MISSALE PARVUM* most helpful. This small, one-volume Missal of 167 pages contains a number of Mass formularies for the various seasons and feastdays, and provides the readings for them as well. To date this Missale Parvum is available only with Latin texts.

---

[128] Cfr. Gen. Instr., n. 211.

# Celebration of Mass Joined with an Hour of the Divine Office

*(All numbers in parenthese refer to pertinent chapters of the General Instruction on the Liturgy of the Hours.)*

The celebration of Holy Mass may be joined with an Hour of the Divine Office where the Liturgy of the Hours is celebrated in choir or in common, or elsewhere, on occasions, provided the faithful participating in the service have been well prepared and there are no pastoral reasons against it. In parish churches this service should be limited to weekdays and the faithful should join in singing/saying the Divine Office as they do in the Mass.

Lauds always precedes the Mass; the Middle Hour and Vespers may either precede or follow the Mass. The Hour and the Mass must always be of the same liturgical Office.

Everything is prepared for Holy Mass as usual; there may be an entrance procession; the priest wears the usual vestments for Mass. The priest and the ministers make the usual reverence to the altar and go to their chairs.

# THE HOUR BEFORE THE MASS

The celebrant may begin the service with either the opening verse and hymn of the Hour or the entrance hymn and greeting of the Mass. The former is appropriate on ferial days; the latter on festive days.

Standing at the chair, the priest blesses himself, saying aloud: O GOD, COME TO MY ASSISTANCE. The people respond: MAKE HASTE TO HELP ME. The priest continues: GLORY BE TO THE FATHER, AND TO THE SON, AND TO THE HOLY SPIRIT, and the people add: AS IT WAS IN THE BEGINNING, IS NOW AND EVER SHALL BE, WORLD WITHOUT END. AMEN. The *ALLELUIA* is added outside of Lent. Then the Hymn of the Hour is sung or recited. Or, if he so chooses, the priest may begin the service in the same way as he begins Mass, making the sign of the cross and saying the greeting as usual. In this latter case the verse of Hour and the hymn of the Hour are omitted. (Cfr. n. 94). The penitential act and, if desired, also the *Kyrie*, are omitted. The priest and the faithful sit, and the three psalms with their antiphons are sung or recited.

After the antiphon of the third psalm, all stand, and the *KYRIE*, if it is added, and the *GLORIA*, if prescribed, are sung or said. The priest then sings or says the opening prayer of the Mass.

The Liturgy of the Word and the Liturgy of the Eucharist are celebrated in the usual manner until after the Communion (Cfr. n. 94).

After the Communion of the faithful, the priest, at the chair, begins the *BENEDICTUS* with its antiphon, at Lauds, or the *MAGNIFICAT* with its antiphon at Vespers. When the canticle and its antiphon are finished, the priest sings or says the prayer after Communion of the Mass. The blessing and the dismissal follow as usual (Cfr. nn. 94 and 96).

When the Middle Hour is joined with Holy Mass, the service begins as described above; only the Hour's psalms with their antiphons are said and the short reading, etc. of the Hour is omitted altogether. (Cfr. n. 95).

The First Vespers of solemnities, Sundays and feasts of the Lord occurring on Sundays, may not be celebrated until after the Mass of the previous day (Cfr. n. 96). Thus, First Vespers of these liturgical days may not be joined with the Mass of the previous day; they would not be of the same Office.

When Lauds is joined with Holy Mass, the priest may, on ferial days, use the Prayers (the Preces) of Lauds in place of the general intercessions, but at the normal place in the Mass (Cfr. n. 94).

# THE HOUR AFTER THE MASS

The priest celebrates Holy Mass as usual until after the prayer after Communion. He then sits at the chair and the three psalms with their antiphons are sung or recited. The opening verse and the hymn of the Hour are omitted.

If the Middle Hour follows the Mass, the priest stands after the last psalm and antiphon and sings or says: LET US PRAY. Then he sings or says the concluding prayer of the Hour. The people respond: AMEN. The blessing and the dismissal are the same as at Mass (Cfr. n. 97).

If Vespers follows Holy Mass, the priest sings or says the prayer after Communion, and then sits at his chair. The psalmody of Vespers is sung or recited. After the last psalm and its antiphon, the priest stands and the *MAGNIFICAT* with its antiphon is sung or said, followed by the concluding prayer of Vespers. The invitation: LET US PRAY, is omitted. Note that the short reading, the Prayers (the Preces) and the OUR FATHER are not said.

The priest blesses and dismisses the assembly as usual (Cfr. n. 97).

During the Hour of the Divine Office, the faithful observe these ceremonies:

all sit during the psalms and antiphons;

all stand for the *BENEDICTUS* or the *MAGNIFICAT* with antiphons, and for the concluding prayer, blessing and dismissal (Cfr. n. 263).

All make the sign of the cross at the opening verse of the Hour, and at the beginning of the *BENEDICTUS* or the *MAGNIFICAT* (Cfr. n. 265).

# Appendix

## A. General rules and requisites for the celebration of Holy Mass.

## 1. VESTURE

"It is clearly evident from the General Instruction (Cfr. n. 299 revised) that the chasuble must always be worn in the celebration of the Mass, as it is the proper vestment of the priest-celebrant" (*Notitiae* 1970, pp. 186-187).

"The vestment common to all ministers of whatever rank is the ALB. The practice of wearing only a stole over the monastic cowl or ordinary clerical garb for concelebration is reproved as an abuse" (Third Instruction, par. 8,c).

The Secretary of the Sacred Congregation for Divine Worship re-affirmed this norm in a reply to queries published in L'Osservatore Romano (August 8, 1974). The queries concerned Masses when traveling, on excursions or camp-outs, at Scout gatherings, etc. The reply stressed that "from this norm the Sacred Congregation for Divine Worship has never derogated, nor does it intend to do so...". The same Sacred Congregation will allow, upon request of the National Episcopal Conference and only in cases of necessity, the use of a full, circular chasuble reaching to the ankles. With this chasuble the ALB may be omitted, and the stole (it must be of the proper liturgical color) is worn over the chasuble. Incidentally this is the only occasion when the stole may be worn outside the chasuble.

The specific vestment, then, of the celebrant at Mass, and of the principal celebrant at concelebration, or at other services connected with the Mass, is the chasuble, unless otherwise indicated (Cfr. Gen. Instr., n. 299 revised). The priest wears the cope in processions and other services, as indicated in the rubrics of each rite (Cfr. Gen. Instr., n. 303).

The specific vestment of the deacon is the DALMATIC (Cfr. Gen. Instr., n. 300).

Each minister, whether deacon, lector or acolyte, must wear the vesture of his order or function, as determined in the General Instruction (nn. 298-299), or, in the case of the extraordinary minister of the Eucharist, as determined by the diocesan Ordinary (Cfr. Study I, Holy Communion, page 3).

The vestment common to all ministers of every rank is the ALB, bound with a cincture at the waist, if necessary. If the alb does not cover the ordinary clothes at the neck, the amice is put on before the alb.

A surplice may replace the alb, except when a dalmatic or a chasuble is worn or when the stole is worn without the chasuble, as at concelebration, and when a stole is worn without the dalmatic, as by a deacon assisting at Mass (Cfr. Gen. Instr., n. 298).

Other ministers wear the alb or the surplice.

The biretta is not mentioned. However, in a

private reply, Archbishop Bugnini stated that it may be used, if the celebrant so wishes.

The Bishops Committee on Liturgy provides the following guidelines:

a) the cincture is worn "unless the alb is made in such a way that it fits the body without a cincture";

b) the amice should be used if the alb "does not completely cover the ordinary clothes at the neck";

c) both the alb and the stole are always worn UNDER the dalmatic or the chasuble. (Newsletter, August, 1970, p. 12).

## 2. COLOR OF VESTMENTS

"Colors in vestments give an effective expression to the celebration of the mysteries of the faith, and in the course of the year, a sense of progress in the Christian life" (Cfr. Gen. Instr., n. 30).

The traditional colors and their use are:

WHITE: in Masses of Easter and Christmas seasons; on feasts and memorials of the Lord, except those of the passion; on feasts and memorials of the Blessed Virgin Mary, the Angels, the Saints who were not martyrs; on All Saints day, the feast of St. John the Evangelist, of St. John the Baptist, of the Chair of Peter and of the Conversion of St. Paul. It is worn during the entire Easter Vigil services.

White vestments may be used in the U.S. in Masses for the Dead.

RED: on Passion (Palm) Sunday for the blessing of palms and the Mass of the passion, on Good Friday and on Pentecost Sunday; in celebrations of the passion; on birthday feasts of the Apostles and Evangelists, and on the feasts of Martyrs.

GREEN: in Masses of ordinary time.

VIOLET: in Lent, in Advent, and it may be used for Masses for the Dead.

BLACK: may be used in Masses for the Dead.

ROSE: may be used on Gaudete and Laetare Sundays (Cfr. Gen. Instr., n. 308).

# 3. USE OF INCENSE

Incense may be used in all forms of the Mass. The incensation may take place:

a) at the entrance procession; b) to incense the altar at the start of Mass; c) at the proclamation of the Gospel; d) at the preparation of the gifts — to incense the altar, the celebrant and the people; e) at the two Consecrations (Cfr. Gen. Instr., n. 235 revised).

When he blesses the incense, the priest simply makes the sign of the cross over it, saying nothing.

# 4. REVERENCES

Three genuflections are normally made during the Mass: after the Consecration of the bread, after the Consecration of the wine, and before saying the words: THIS IS THE LAMB OF GOD..., at Communion time.

If the tabernacle is in the altar area, a genuflection is made before the Mass begins and before leaving the sanctuary at the end of Mass. If the tabernacle door is opened for Communion of the people, a genuflection is made before closing the door after the distribution. When passing before the tabernacle, the minister makes a genuflection each time.

A profound bow is made by the celebrant: a) on entering the sanctuary, when there is no tabernacle nearby; b) at the prayer, ALMIGHTY GOD, CLEANSE MY HEART. . . . , should he read the Gospel; c) at the words, BY THE POWER OF THE HOLY SPIRIT. . . . , in the profession of faith; d) at the prayer, LORD GOD, WE ASK YOU. . . . , before the Lavabo; e) at the prayer, ALMIGHTY GOD, WE PRAY. . . . . , in the Eucharistic Prayer I.

A profound bow is made by the concelebrants: a) when entering or leaving the sanctuary, when there is no tabernacle nearby; b) at the words, BY THE POWER OF THE HOLY SPIRIT. . . . , in the profession of faith; c) when the principal celebrant genuflects after each Consecration; d) when saying the prayer, ALMIGHTY GOD, WE PRAY. . . . . , in Eucharistic Prayer I.

A profound bow is made by the deacon: a) when entering or leaving the sanctuary, when there is no tabernacle nearby; b) when he asks the celebrant's blessing before the Gospel; c) when saying the words, BY THE POWER OF THE HOLY SPIRIT, in the profession of faith.

A slight bow is made by the celebrant when he pronounces the very words of Christ at the Consecrations (Cfr. Gen. Instr., no. 233-234).

A bow of the head is made when the Holy Name of Jesus is mentioned in the texts of the Mass; also at mention of the Trinity, of the name of the

Blessed Virgin Mary and of the Saint in whose honor the Mass is celebrated (Cfr. Gen. Instr., n. 234, a, revised).

# 5. POSITION OF PRIESTS FINGERS

"After the Consecration, the celebrant need not join the thumbs and forefingers; if there is any fragment of the Host on his fingers, the priest purifies his fingers over the paten" (Second Instruction, n. 12).

This provision eliminates any scrupulosity about forms of reverence to the Eucharistic Species and indicates a simple rule, namely, if any fragments cling to the fingers, he merely purifies his fingers by rubbing them together over the paten.

# 6. NO WINE IN CHALICE

Should the priest, after the Consecration or even when he receives Communion, notice that water and not wine was in the chalice, he pours the water into a glass or other container and then puts some wine and a little water into the chalice and repeats that part of the words of institution which pertains to the Consecration of the wine. There is no need to repeat the Consecration of the bread. (Cfr. Gen. Instr., n. 286).

# 7. ACTIONS AND POSTURES

At their meeting in November 1969, the National Conference of Catholic Bishops voted that in general the directives of the Roman Missal concerning the posture of the congregation at Mass should be left unchanged, but that n. 21 of the General Instruction should be so adapted that the people kneel beginning after the singing of the Sanctus until after the AMEN of the Eucharistic Prayer, that is, before the Lord's Prayer (Newsletter, Apr.-May 1970, p. 8).

# 8. SILENCE

At the proper times, all should observe a reverent silence. Through it the faithful are not only not considered as extraneous or dumb spectators at the liturgical service, but are associated more intimately in the mystery that is being celebrated, thanks to that interior disposition which derives from the Word of God that they have heard, from the songs and prayers that have been uttered, and from spiritual union with the priest in the parts that he says or sings himself (Instr. on Music in the Liturgy, n. 17).

# 9. CONCELEBRATION

Bishops and competent superiors should make sure that the concelebration in communities and in priests' residences is done with dignity and true piety. In order to achieve this purpose and the spiritual good of all, the freedom of the concelebrants must be respected and internal and external participation fostered through a genuine and integral ordering of the concelebration according to the norms of the General Instruction of the Roman Missal. Care should be taken that each part of the Mass is carried out according to its own nature, the distinction of offices and function is respected, and the role of music and silence is considered.

Those priests who celebrate for the people and concelebrate another Mass may not accept another stipend for the concelebrated Mass.

Although concelebration is the most important form of Eucharistic celebration in communities, even celebration without the participation of the faithful "remains the center of the life of the entire Church and the heart of priestly existence.

Every priest must be afforded the opportunity to celebrate individually, and to foster such freedom everything should be provided which will facilitate this celebration: time, place, server, etc. (Declaration or Concelebration, n. 3, a-b-c).

## 10. CONVENTUAL MASS

Members of Chapters and members of communities of any religious institute of perfection who are obliged by their office to celebrate for the pastoral good of the faithful may concelebrate the conventual or community Mass on the same day. Eucharistic concelebration in communities is to be greatly esteemed. Concelebration signifies and strengthens the fraternal bond of priests among themselves and with the entire community. In this manner of celebrating the Sacrifice, with all participating actively and consciously, in their own proper way, the action of the entire community and the manifestation of the Church are more clearly made visible in the unity of sacrifice and priesthood, in the one act of thanksgiving around the one altar (Declaration on Concelebration, n. 1. Cfr. Gen. Instr., n. 76 revised, and IEW, n. 47).

# 11. A PROBLEM AND ONE POSSIBLE SOLUTION

When Mass is celebrated at an altar which does not face the congregation, how does the priest show the Host and the chalice with the Precious Blood to the people after the Consecrations without resorting to the former elevation? One solution to the problem was suggested by the liturgical Commission of the diocese of Lecce (in Italy) and was published in LITURGIA, the monthly liturgical review published in Rome.

After the Consecration of the bread, the priest takes the Host, holding the paten underneath, turns towards the faithful and shows them the Body of the Lord for their adoration. Then he places the paten on the corporal and the Host on the paten, and makes a genuflection. Likewise with the chalice after the Consecration of the wine. The priest takes the chalice with the Precious Blood in it with both hands, turns towards the faithful and shows them the chalice of the Lord's Blood for their adoration. He rests the chalice again on the corporal, covers it, if the pall is used, and makes his genuflection.

# 12. TONE OF VOICE OF CONCELEBRANTS

Since it is not intended that the recitation of the appointed texts of the Eucharistic prayer (at concelebration) should be choral, the General Instruction is explicit: only the principal celebrant should speak loudly enough to be heard by the people; the others should use a tone sufficiently low so that the principal celebrant will be clearly understood. (Cfr. Newsletter, February 1973, p. 4).

# 13. THE PRESIDENTIAL PRAYERS

The nature of the presidential prayers demands that they be spoken in a loud and clear voice so that everyone present may hear and pay attention. While the priest is speaking, there should be no other prayer or song, and the organ and other musical instruments should be silent.

Among the prayers assigned to the priest, the Eucharistic prayer has precedence; it is the high point of the whole celebration. Next are: the opening prayer or collect, the prayer over the gifts, and the prayer after Communion. (Cfr. Gen. Instr., nn. 10 and 12).

## B. Selected Excerpts from Official Documents and Instructions
## The Third Instruction on the Correct Application of the Constitution on the Sacred Liturgy.

# 14. ADAPTATION

The wide choice of texts and the flexibility of the rubrics makes it possible to adapt the celebration to the circumstances, the mentality and the preparation of the assembly. Thus there is no need to resort to arbitrary adaptations, which would only weaken the impact of the liturgy. The possibilities offered by the Church's reforms can make the celebration vital, moving and spiritually effective. (Introduction)

# 15. SACRED CHARACTER OF THE LITURGY

The simplification (of liturgical formulas) must not go beyond certain limits, for otherwise the liturgy would be deprived of its sacred signs and of its appeal to the senses. These are necessary to make the mystery of salvation really effective in the Christian community and, by means of catechetical instruction, to make it rightly understood under the visible symbols.

Liturgical reform is not at all synonymous with so-called desacralization and is not intended as an occasion for what is called secularization. Thus the liturgy must keep a dignified and sacred character.

The effectiveness of liturgical actions does not consist in the continual search for new rites or simpler forms, but in an ever deeper insight into the Word of God and the mystery which is celebrated. The priest will assure the presence of God and His mystery in the celebration by following the rites of the Church rather than his own preferences.

The priest should keep in mind that by imposing his own personal restoration of sacred rites, he is offending the rights of the faithful and is introducing individualism and idiosyncracy into the celebrations which belong to the whole Church.

The ministry of the priest is the ministry of the Church, and it can be exercised only in obedience, in hierarchical fellowship, and in devotion to the service of God and of his brothers. The hierarchical structure of the liturgy, its sacramental value, and the respect due to the community of God's people require that the priest exercise his liturgical service as a "faithful minister and steward of the mysteries of God" (I. Cor. 4,1). He should not add any rite which is not contained in the liturgical books. (Par. 1).

# 16. ONE ACT OF WORSHIP

The Liturgy of the Word prepares the assembly and leads them to the celebration of the Eucharist. Thus the two parts of the Mass form one act of worship, and may not be celebrated separately, at different times or in different places. (Par. 2,b).

# 17. LITURGICAL TEXTS

The liturgical texts composed by the Church also deserve great respect. No one may make changes, substitutions, additions or deletions in them. (Par. 3).

This rule applies especially to the 'Ordo Missae'. The formulas which it contains, in the official translations, may never be altered, not even when Mass is sung. However, some parts of the rite, such as: the penitential rite, the Eucharistic prayer, the acclamations of the people, the final blessing, can be chosen from various alternative formulas, as indicated for each rite. (Par. 3,a).

Great freedom of choice is given for selecting the orations; especially on weekdays 'per annum' these may be taken from any one of the 34 Mass formularies, from the Masses for special intentions, or from the votive Masses. (Par. 3,d).

With regard to the readings, besides those indicated for each Sunday, feast and ferial day, a wide choice of readings is given for the celebration of the Sacraments and for special circumstances. When Mass is celebrated with special groups, texts which are suited to the group may be chosen, provided they are from an approved lectionary. (Par. 3, e).

During the celebration of the Mass, the priest may say a few words to the people: at the beginning, before the readings, the preface, the prayer after Communion, and before the dismissal. (Par. 3,f).

## 18. EUCHARISTIC PRAYER

The Eucharistic prayer is the prayer of the priest; of all parts of the Mass, it is that which belongs especially to him alone, because of his office. Thus it is not permitted to have some part of it read by a minister of lower rank, by the assembly or by a lay person. This would be against the hierarchical structure of the liturgy in which everyone must take part by doing solely and totally what is required of him. Thus the priest alone must say the whole Eucharistic prayer. (Par. 4).

## 19. ARTICLES USED IN WORSHIP

Things which are used for worship must always be of high quality, durable, and suited to liturgical use. Thus common or household articles may not be used in the liturgy. (Par. 8,a).

## 20. PLACE OF CELEBRATION

The Eucharist is normally celebrated in church. The Ordinary, within his own jurisdiction, will decide when there is real necessity which permits celebrating outside the church. In such cases, careful attention should be given to the choice of a place and a table which are fitting for the Eucharistic sacrifice. As far as possible, dining halls and tables on which meals are eaten should not be used for the celebration. (Par. 9).

The Instruction on Sacramental Communion and Commentary

## 21. COMMUNION FROM THE CHALICE

Among the ways of distribution given by the Instruction of the Roman Missal, the reception of Communion by drinking from the chalice itself certainly has pre-eminence. However this method should only be chosen when everything can be carried out in an orderly fashion and without any danger of irreverence towards the Blood of the Lord. If there are other priests present, or deacons or (instituted) acolytes, they should therefore be asked to help by presenting the chalice. On the other hand, it does not seem that manner of distribution should be approved in which the chalice is passed from one to another, or in which the communicants came up directly to take the chalice themselves and receive the Blood of the Lord. When the ministers above are not available, then if the communicants are few in number and Communion is taken directly from the chalice, the same priest should distribute Communion first under the species of bread and afterwards under the species of wine.

Otherwise the rite of Communion under both kinds by intinction is to be preferred in order that practical difficulties may be avoided and that due reverence might the more aptly be given to the Sacrament. In this way access to Communion under both kinds is offered more easily and safely to the faithful, whatever their age or condition, and at the same time the fullness of the sign is preserved. (Part 2, Drinking from the Chalice).

## 22. MORE ON COMMUNION FROM THE CHALICE

Communion from the chalice should be avoided when large crowds are to receive Communion. The reason is that it would be difficult for the rite to be carried out with respect, order, dignity and piety, even if there were more priests or deacons or (instituted) acolytes 'presenting the chalice'. The presence of an adequate minister to present the chalice is absolutely necessary; it is categorically excluded, therefore, that the faithful should receive Communion at the chalice by themselves, or that they should pass the chalice to one another, a method alien to the liturgy, even in the 'Supper' of the separated brethren. (Commentary, n. 4,b).

## 23. ACOLYTE AS MINISTER OF THE EUCHARIST

It should be noted that by "acolyte" is meant not an assistant filling the function of an acolyte, but a young seminarian of the theological course, who has received the acolyte 'order', as a result of which he is designated to carry and hand the Eucharist to the faithful, to help the ordinary minister, who is the priest or the deacon. Commentary, n. 4,b).

Instruction on Eucharistic Worship

## 24. ROLE OF THE PEOPLE OF GOD

It should be made clear that all who gather for the Eucharist constitute that holy people which, together with the ministers, plays its part in the sacred action. It is indeed the priest alone who, acting in the person of Christ, consecrates the bread and wine, but the role of the faithful in the Eucharist is to recall the passion, resurrection and glorification of the Lord, to give thanks to God, and to offer the immaculate Victim not only through the hands of the priest, but also together with him; and finally, by receiving the Body of Christ, to perfect that communion with God and among themselves which should be the product of participation in the Sacrifice of the Mass. For the faithful achieve a more perfect participation in the Mass when, with proper dispositions, they receive the

Body of the Lord sacramentally in the Mass itself, in obedience to His words: Take and eat. (Par. 12).

## 25. SIMULTANEOUS MASSES

In liturgical celebrations, the community should not be disrupted or be distracted from its common purpose. Care then must be taken not to have two liturgical celebrations at the same time in the same church, since it distracts the people's attention.

This is above all true of the celebration of the Eucharist. That is why that disruption of the congregation is to be assiduously avoided, which, when Mass is celebrated with the people on Sundays and feastdays, is caused by the simultaneous celebration of Masses in the same church.

As far as possible it should be avoided on other days as well. (Par. 17).

## 26. CARE TO BE TAKEN BY MINISTERS

The people have the right to be nourished by the proclamation of the Word of God and by the minister's explanation of it. Priests, then, will not only give the homily whenever it is prescribed or seems suitable, but will ensure that whatever they or the ministers say or sing will be so clear that the faithful will be able to hear it easily and grasp its meaning; and they will in fact be spontaneously drawn to respond and participate. The ministers should undergo a careful preparation for this, above all in seminaries and religious houses. (Par. 20).

## 27. ANTICIPATED MASSES AND COMMUNION

In these cases (of anticipating the Sunday or Holy Day Masses on the previous evening) the Mass celebrated is that assigned in the calendar to Sunday (or Holy Day); the homily and the general intercessions are not to be omitted. (Par. 28, 3).

The faithful who begin the Sunday or Holy Day of Obligation on the preceding evening may go to Communion at that Mass even if they have already received Communion in the morning. (Par. 28, 6).

## 28. CELEBRANT IS MINISTER OF COMMUNION

It should belong to the celebrant priest above all to distribute Communion; nor should the Mass continue until the Communion of the faithful is over. Other priests or deacons will help the priest, if need be. (Par. 31, 3).

## 29. REVERENCE BEFORE RECEIVING COMMUNION

In accordance with the custom of the Church, Communion may be received by the faithful either standing or kneeling. . . . . The faithful should willingly adopt the method indicated by their pastors, so that Communion may truly be a sign of the brotherly union of all those who share in the same table of the Lord. (Par. 34,a).

When the faithful communicate kneeling, no other sign of reverence toward the Blessed Sacrament is required, since kneeling is itself a sign of adoration.

When they receive standing, it is strongly recommended that, coming up in procession, they should make a sign of reverence before receiving the Blessed Sacrament. This should be done at the right time and place, so that the order of people going to and from Communion may not be disrupted. (Par. 34,b).

## 30. ROLE OF PRIEST

In the celebration of the Eucharist, priests also are deputed to perform a specific function by reason of a special Sacrament, namely, Holy Orders. For they, too, "as ministers of the sacred mysteries, especially in the sacrifice of the Mass . . . , act in the person of Christ in a special way". It is, therefore, fitting that, by reason of the sign, they participate in the Eucharist by exercising the order proper to them, by celebrating or concelebrating the Mass and not by limiting themselves to communicating like the laity. (Par. 43).

## 31. DAILY MASS

In the mystery of the Eucharistic sacrifice, in which the priest exercises his highest function, the work of the redemption is continually accomplished. Daily celebration of Mass, therefore, is most earnestly recommended, since, even if the faithful cannot be present, it remains an action of Christ and of the Church, an action in which the priest is always acting for the salvation of the people. (Par. 44).

## 32. UNAUTHORIZED CHANGES

Especially in the celebration of the Eucharist, no one, not even a priest, may on his own authority add, omit, or change anything in the liturgy. Only the supreme authority of the Church, and, according to the provisions of the law, the Bishop and the episcopal conference, may do this. Priests, should, therefore, ensure that they so preside over the celebration of the Eucharist that the faithful know that they are taking part not in a rite established on private initiative, but in the Church's public worship, the regulation of which was entrusted by Christ to the Apostles and their successors. (Par. 45).

> Letter to the Presidents of the National Conferences of Bishops Concerning Eucharistic Prayers

## 33. ORDER OF EUCHARISTIC PRAYER

The four Eucharistic prayers presently appearing in the revised Roman Missal remain, and no other Eucharistic prayers composed without the express approval or permission of the Holy See may be used.

The Holy See is motivated by a pastoral love of unity in reserving to itself the right of regulating so important a matter as the order of the Eucharistic prayer. (Par. 6).

# 34. NATURE OF EUCHARISTIC PRAYER

By its very nature the Eucharistic prayer is the center of the entire celebration, and a prayer of thanksgiving and sanctification, whereby the entire congregation of believers join Christ in acknowledging the works of God and offering the sacrifice. This prayer is proclaimed by the presiding priest. He expresses the voice of God as it is addressed to the people, and the voice of the people as they turn to God. He alone should proclaim this prayer, while those assembled for the sacred celebration observe a reverent silence. (Par. 8, part 1).

To allow those participating to praise God and give Him even greater thanks, the revised Roman Missal already contains a great number of prefaces, derived from the older tradition of the Roman Church or newly composed. In this way the different aspects of the mystery of salvation will be emphasized, and there will be richer themes of thanksgiving. (Par. 8, part 2).

To this end, the presiding priest has the faculty of briefly introducing the Eucharistic prayer. He can thereby suggest reasons for giving thanks which are then and there meaningful to the particular group of people. The community will then be able to feel its own life is an intimate part of the history of salvation, and so draw greater benefits from the Eucharistic celebration. (Par. 8, part 3).

# 35. PRAYER OF THE WHOLE CHURCH

The ecclesial dimension of the Eucharistic prayer should be considered paramount. While it is within such a celebration that the unity of all believers who form one body in Christ is both expressed and brought about, the celebration of Mass is, in itself, a profession of faith whereby the entire Church recognizes and expresses her own nature. Nowhere is this more apparent than in the Eucharistic prayer, for it is not just an individual person, nor even the local community, but "the one and only Catholic Church, existing in the local chuches" that addresses itself to God.

Whenever Eucharistic prayers are used without any approval of the Church's authority, unrest and even dissensions arise, not only among priests, but within the communities themselves, even though the Eucharist should be a "sign of unity, and the bond of charity". Many people complain about the overly subjective quality of such texts, and participants have a right to make such a complaint. Otherwise, the Eucharistic prayer, to which they give their assent in the AMEN they proclaim, becomes disorderly, or is imbued with the personal feelings of the person who either composes or says it.

Hence it is necessary to demand that only those Eucharistic prayers be used which have been approved by the lawful authority of the Church, for they clearly and fully manifest the sentiments of the Church. (Par. 11).

# 36. ADMONITIONS

Among the possibilities for further accomodating any individual celebration, it is important to consider the admonitions, the homily, and the general intercessions.

First of all are the admonitions. These enable the people to be drawn into a fuller understanding of the sacred action, or any of its parts, and lead them into a true spirit of participation. The General Instruction of the Roman Missal entrusts the more important admonitions to the priest for preparation and use. He may introduce the Mass to the people before the celebration begins, during the Liturgy of the Word prior to the actual readings, and in the Eucharistic prayer before the preface; he may also conclude the entire sacred action before the dismissal. The Order of Mass provides others as well, which are important to certain portions of the rite, such as during the penitential rite, or before the Lord's Prayer. By their very nature these brief admonitions do not require that everyone use them in the form in which they appear in the Missal. Provision can be made in certain cases that they be adapted to some degree to the varying circumstances of the community. In all cases it is well to remember the nature of an admonition, and not make them into a sermon or homily; care should be taken to keep them brief and not too wordy, for otherwise they become tedious. (Par. 14).

## 37. HOMILY

In addition to these admonitions, the homily must be kept in mind, for it is part of the liturgy itself. It proclaims the Word of God in the liturgical gathering for the community assembled. It explains that Word of God in view of the total celebration respecting the ability of the people to understand and in terms of their daily life. (Par. 15).

## 38. SILENCE
*(See No. 8 above)*

A sacred silence must be observed at the proper times, in order that the texts may achieve their full effect and enable the greatest possible spiritual benefits to be gained. As an integral part of the liturgical action, the nature of this silence and the time when it is introduced allow individuals to become recollected, or to meditate briefly upon what they have heard, or to pray and praise God in their hearts. (Par. 18).

### C. Other Matters

## 39. MINISTRIES IN THE MASS

Everyone in the Eucharistic assembly has the right and duty to take his own part according to the diversity of orders and functions. In exercising his function, everyone, whether minister or layman, should do that and only that which belongs to him, so that in the liturgy the Church may be seen in its variety of orders and ministries. (Gen. Instr., n. 58).

# 40. ACCLAMATION AFTER CONSECRATION

If none of the faithful is present to make the acclamation after the Consecration, it is omitted along with the invitation. (Newsletter, Oct.-Nov. 1969, p. 7).

# 41. INTRODUCTION TO LORD'S PRAYER

The words which introduce the Lord's Prayer in the Mass may be varied at the discretion of the priest in such a way as to introduce the whole Communion rite of the Mass, provided this is done briefly and simply. (Newsletter, May 1973, p. 2).

# 42. COMMUNION IN THE HAND

Pope Paul has ruled out any change in the traditional manner of giving Holy Communion, unless a two-thirds majority of the members of the National Bishops Conference so request. Our National Conference of Catholic Bishops has made no such request. The present usage, prescribed by long custom and repeatedly re-affirmed, arises from a better understanding of the Eucharist, as well as a sense of humility, and must be retained; so that the minister properly places the Host on the tongue of the communicants. Permission to do otherwise may not be given even by the Ordinary. (Notitiae 1972, p. 343. Also *Notitiae* 1969, p. 347, and Newsletter, June-July, 1969, p. 4).

# 43. SIGN OF PEACE

The introduction: Let us offer each other. . . . . This is one of the presidential interventions for which the Order of Mass supplies definite texts.

Father G. Fontaine, a Consultor for the Sacred Congregation for Divine Worship, offers this opinion in *Notitiae* (1972, p. 152): "I believe that it must be clearly established that the introductory texts in the Ordo Missae are not "ne varietur" texts, as the orations, prefaces, and Eucharistic prayers; but they are models or examples for inspiration to be adapted to the genius of the vernacular and the needs of the diverse assemblies. . . . Even if the texts published in the Ordo Missae are good, their repetition at every Mass quickly causes them to lose their significance and produces boredom, routine, and liturgical sclerosis. To make them efficacious it is sufficient if they vary somewhat according to the assembly, feast, and particular circumstances".

Newsletter adds this comment (July-Aug. 1972, p. 8): "Giving due respect to the established text and the official rite, the diverse interventions give opportunity for the president and/or the deacon to personalize the liturgical action provided that the interventions have been prepared by a study of the text and by personal prayer, and that due respect has been given to the genre and to the function of the interventions — as each plays a unique role in the liturgical action".

When the sign of peace is given, there is no standard rule or pattern. Local custom should prevail; however, the double hand-clasp seems more significant than the hand-shake. If a greeting or a prayer is added to the gesture, it should be done very quietly: Peace be with you; Grace and peace be yours; The God of love and peace be with you. (Additional suggestions can be found in Newsletter, Jan.-Feb. 1971, p. 6; and in *Notitiae*, 1973, p. 146).

# 44. EXTRAORDINARY MINISTER OF THE EUCHARIST

The role of 'The Extraordinary Minister of the Eucharist' is described in detail in Study I — Holy Communion, issued by the Bishops Committee on the Liturgy (pp. 11-17). Study I provides the following guidelines:

a) The special minister of the Eucharist does not assist the priest at the altar during Mass as would the deacon. He may have an assigned place and may enter with the other ministers of the Mass in the entrance procession.

b) The special minister does not wear the stole — the vestment restricted to the priest and deacon, but should be dressed neatly according to local usage.

c) The special minister is qualified to assist the celebrating priest to distribute Holy Communion during Mass, when a very lengthy distribution of the Sacrament cannot otherwise be avoided.

d) The special minister enters the sanctuary during the breaking of the bread and stands near the altar. After his own Communion, the priest gives Communion (under both kinds) to the special minister, and then gives the ciborium to him; and both proceed to distribute the Sacrament.

e) In giving Communion the special minister holds the consecrated particle a little elevated and says: THE BODY OF CHRIST, to which the communicant responds: AMEN, before receiving.

f) After Communion the special minister returns to his place.

g) The special minister may give Holy Communion to himself only outside of Mass, and to others outside of Mass in the absence of an ordinary minister, or if the latter is impeded by age, bad health or other pastoral ministry. In this case the special minister should follow the rite provided in the appendix of Study I[129] or in the ritual[130].

---

[129] Study I, page 40.
[130] E.R. nn. 26-53.

# Official Sources Used

*MISSALE ROMANUM:* Lectionary ............ 1969
                   Sacramentary ...... 1970
Liturgy of the Hours ..................................... 1971
Rite of Anointing and Pastoral Care
   of the Sick ............................................... 1972
Holy Communion and Eucharistic Devotion
   Outside of Mass ....................................... 1973
Constitution on the Sacred Liturgy ............ 1963
Second Instruction on the Correct
   Implementation of the Constitution
   on the Sacred Liturgy ............................. 1967
Third Instruction on the Correct
   Application of the Constitution
   on the Sacred Liturgy ............................. 1970
Instruction on Eucharistic Worship ............ 1967
Instruction on Sacramental Communion ...... 1970
Notification on the Roman Missal, Liturgy
   of the Hours and the Calendar .............. 1971
Declaration on Concelebration ...................... 1972
*Ministeria Quaedam* ......................................... 1972
Eucharistic Prayers, Letter on ...................... 1973
Instruction on Facilitating Sacramental
   Communion in Particular Cirmustances .. 1973
Instruction on Music in the Liturgy ............ 1967
Eucharistic Prayers for Concelebration ........ 1973
*NOTITIAE* — monthly bulletin of the
   Sacred Congregation for
   Divine Worship .......................... Vatican City
NEWSLETTER — monthly release of the
   Bishops Committee on the
   Liturgy ................................. Washington, D.C.

# Index

| | |
|---|---|
| Ablutions at Mass | 50 |
| Ablutions by deacon | 65 |
| Ablutions at Mass in private | 113 |
| Acclamation at consecration | 143 |
| Acclamation at Embolism | 46, 95 |
| Acclamation omitted | 143 |
| Acolytes | 71 |
| Acolytes ministers of Eucharist | 134 |
| Actions and Postures | 124 |
| Adaptations | 128 |
| Admonitions | 141 |
| Alb | 119, 120 |
| *Alleluia* | 18, 107 |
| *Alleluia* should be sung | 20 |
| Altar | 2 |
| Altar preparation of | 25 |
| Altar incensing of | 30 |
| Altarboys, see Acolytes | |
| Altarbreads, larger | 87 |
| Altarbreads, not broken | 33 |
| *Ambo* | 2 |
| Amice | 121 |
| Antiphon, Introit | 6, 8, 105 |
| Anticipated Masses | 136 |
| Arbitrary adaptations | 138 |
| Articles Used in Worship | 131 |
| Aspergill | 11 |
| | |
| Basin/towel | 3, 83 |
| Benedictus | 117 |
| Biretta | 120 |
| Blessing omitted | 113 |
| Blessing/sprinkling holy water | 11 |
| Blessings, Solemn | 53 |
| Book of Gospels | 6, 20 |
| Bow, profound, at Creed | 20, 107 |
| Bows | 123 |

| | |
|---|---|
| Breaking of bread | 47, 96 |
| Candlebearers | 5, 22 |
| Care to be taken by ministers | 135 |
| Casket, incensing of | 30 |
| Celebrant at chair | 7, 85 |
| Celebrant at altar | 28, 86 |
| Celebrant at sign of peace | 46, 96 |
| Celebrant incensing of | 30 |
| Celebrant to distribute Communion | 136 |
| Chair for celebrant | 1 |
| Chairs for concelebrants | 84 |
| Chalice at altar | 25, 51, 103 |
| Chalice at credence | 3 |
| Chalice Communion from | 132 |
| Chalice cleansing of | 50, 99 |
| Chasuble required | 120 |
| Ciborium | 28, 50 |
| Cincture | 121 |
| Colors of vestments | 121 |
| Communicants, proper | 40 |
| Communion Rite | 45, 95, 110 |
| Communion in the Hand | 143 |
| Communion of celebrant | 48 |
| Communion of concelebrants | 96ff |
| Communion of deacon | 49, 65, 99 |
| Communion of faithful | 48, 55ff |
| Communion of minister | 49 |
| Communion of acolytes | 75 |
| Communion under both kinds | 55ff |
| Communion from chalice | 132 |
| Communion by intinction | 57 |
| Communion with silver tubes | 59 |
| Communion spoon | 59 |
| Communion Antiphon | 50, 112 |
| Communion hymn | 50 |
| Communion minister of - required | 50, 134 |
| Communion paten | 55, 76 |
| Concelebration | 81, 125 |
| Concelebration preparations for | 83 |
| Concelebration stipend for | 126 |

| | |
|---|---|
| Concluding prayer of the Hour | 118 |
| Conclusion of prayers | 13, 52 |
| Consecration | 36, 89 |
| Consecration incense at | 79 |
| Contributions, weekly | 27 |
| Conventual Mass | 126 |
| Corporal | 3, 27, 51, 108 |
| Crossbearer | 5 |
| Crucifix | 2 |
| Cruets | 2, 75 |
| | |
| Daily Mass | 137 |
| Dalmatic | 62, 120 |
| Deacon | 61 |
| Deacon duties of - by another | 83 |
| Deacon vesture of | 61 |
| Dismissal | 52, 113 |
| Dismissal omitted | 52, 100, 114 |
| Divine Office, Mass joined with | 115 |
| Doxology | 38, 90 |
| Doxology Deacon at | 65 |
| Doxology by celebrants alone | 90 |
| | |
| Elevation | 37 |
| Entrance Hymn | 6, 116 |
| Entrance procession | 6 |
| Eucharist, minister of - req. | 133 |
| Eucharistic Prayer | 131 |
| Eucharistic style of delivery | 32 |
| Eucharistic by celeb. alone | 131, 139 |
| Eucharistic I (Roman Canon) | 39, 90 |
| Eucharistic II | 41, 92 |
| Eucharistic III | 43, 93 |
| Eucharistic IV | 44, 94 |
| Eucharistic parts by concel. | 91ff |
| Eucharistic Prayers | 139 |
| Exhortations | 141 |
| Extraordinary min. of Euch. | 145 |
| | |
| Faithful, role of | 134 |
| Fingers not joined | 33, 124 |
| First Vespers | 117 |

| | |
|---|---:|
| Foot of altar prayers | 103 |
| Fragments | 50 |
| Funeral Mass, homily at | 23 |
| General Intercessions | 24, 107 |
| Genuflections | 122 |
| Gestures should be natural | 36 |
| Gifts, procession of | 27 |
| *Gloria* | 12, 105 |
| Gospel by deacon | 20, 63 |
| Gospel by another priest | 21 |
| Gospel by celebrant | 22 |
| Gospel at Mass in private | 107 |
| Gospel in concelebration | 86 |
| Greeting | 8, 105 |
| Handbell | 3, 37 |
| Hanc igitur, proper | 40 |
| Holy Name, bow at | 123 |
| Homily | 22, 142 |
| Homily no dialogue at | 23 |
| Hour of Divine Office | 115 |
| Hymn, entrance | 6 |
| Hymn, of the Hour | 116 |
| Incense, Use of | 122 |
| Incense at start of Mass | 7 |
| Incense at Gospel | 20, 78 |
| Incense at preparation | 30, 79 |
| Incense at consecrations | 75 |
| *Ite, Missa est*, omitted | 113 |
| Intinction, Communion by | 57, 99 |
| Introductory Rites | 5, 84, 103 |
| Introduction to Lord's Prayer | 143 |
| Kneeling at Mass | 34 |
| *Kyrie* | 10, 105 |
| *Kyrie* omitted | 11 |
| Lamb of God | 47, 112 |
| Language at Private Mass | 101 |
| Larger altarbread | 87 |
| Lauds, Mass joined with | 115 |

| | |
|---|---|
| Lavabo | 30, 108 |
| Lectionary | 2, 83, 103 |
| Lectionary use of | 15 |
| Lector | 16, 67 |
| Liturgy of the Word | 15, 86, 105 |
| Liturgy of the Eucharist | 25, 86, 108 |
| Liturgical Texts | 130 |
| Lord's Prayer | 46, 95, 110 |
| Lord's Prayer introduction to | 143 |
| | |
| *Magnificat* | 117, 118 |
| Manner of carrying book | 5 |
| Mass with a congregation | 1 |
| Mass without a congregation | 101 |
| Mass concelebrated | 81 |
| Mass in private | 101 |
| Mass joined with Divine Office | 115 |
| Mass daily | 137 |
| Minister of the Eucharist | 134, 145 |
| Ministries in the Mass | 142 |
| Missale Parvum | 114 |
| | |
| Names of Pope/Bishop | 38 |
| Nature of Eucharistic Prayer | 139 |
| Nuptial Mass, homily at | 23 |
| | |
| Official Sources | 147 |
| One Act of Worship | 130 |
| Opening Prayer of Mass | 12, 85, 105 |
| Opening Verse of Hour | 116 |
| Order of procession | 5 |
| Order of Eucharistic Prayer | 138 |
| | |
| Paten, Marger - for altarbreads | 25, 29 |
| Paten, Communion | 55 |
| Peace, sign of | 46, 96, 144 |
| Peace-greeting | 46, 96 |
| Penitential act | 8, 85 |
| Penitential at Mass in private | 105 |
| Penitential omitted | 11 |
| Place of celebration | 132 |
| Position of fingers | 124 |

| | |
|---|---|
| Pray, Brethren | 31, 87 |
| Pray, Brother | 108 |
| Prayer of the Whole Church | 140 |
| Prayer, the Eucharistic | 131 |
| Prayer, before Communion | 47, 96, 112 |
| Prayer, of the faithful | 24, 107 |
| Prayer, for peace | 46, 95, 110 |
| Prayer, over gifts | 31, 87, 110 |
| Prayer, over the People | 54 |
| Prayer, after Communion | 52, 100, 113 |
| Preces of Lauds | 117 |
| Preface | 33-34 |
| Preface inseparable | 44 |
| Preparation of altar | 25, 86 |
| Preparatory Rites | 28 |
| Presidential Prayers | 128 |
| Priests, role of | 137 |
| Procession of gifts | 27 |
| Procession order of | 5 |
| Profession of faith | 23 |
| Psalmist | 18 |
| Psalms of the Hour | 116, 117 |
| Purificator | 3, 48, 97 |
| | |
| Responsorial psalm | 18, 68, 107 |
| Reverences | 122 |
| Reverence before Communion | 136 |
| Right to Mass individually | 101 |
| Role of the People of God | 134 |
| Roles of participants | 142 |
| Role of the priest | 137 |
| Rules and Requisites | 119 |
| | |
| Sacred Character of Liturgy | 129 |
| Salt, vessel of | 11 |
| Sanctuary for ministers only | 32 |
| Sanctus | 36, 88, 110 |
| Scripture Readings | 15 |
| Sequences | 18 |
| Servers, see Acolytes | |
| Sign of peace | 46, 96, 144 |

| | |
|---|---|
| Silence, Sacred | 125, 142 |
| Simultaneous Masses | 135 |
| Sources, Official | 147 |
| Stole | 3, 82, 120 |
| Stole worn under chasuble | 121 |
| Surplice may replace alb. | 120 |
| | |
| Thurifer | 77 |
| Thurifer at Gospel | 78 |
| Thurifer at preparation of gifts | 79 |
| Thurifer at consecrations | 79 |
| Tone of voice | 127 |
| Tongue, Communion on the | 49, 143 |
| | |
| Unauthorized changes | 138 |
| Universal Prayer | 24, 107 |
| Universal forms of | 107 |
| Use of Incense | 122 |
| | |
| Variations, unauthorized | 138 |
| Veil, chalice | 74 |
| Veneration of the altar | 7, 85, 105 |
| Vessels for Communion | 49 |
| Vessels, cleansing of | 51 |
| Vesture | 119 |
| Vesture of celebrant | 3 |
| Vesture of principal celebr. | 82 |
| Vesture of deacon | 3 |
| Vesture of ministers | 5 |
| Vesture of concelebrants | 82 |
| Vesture colors of | 121 |
| Voice, Tone of | 127 |
| | |
| Water instead of wine | 124 |